002027171

the outsourcing dilemma

the outsourcing dilemma

● ●

the search for competitiveness

J. Brian Heywood

FINANCIAL TIMES
Prentice Hall

An imprint of **Pearson Education**

London · New York · San Francisco · Toronto · Sydney
Tokyo · Singapore · Hong Kong · Cape Town · Madrid
Paris · Milan · Munich · Amsterdam

PEARSON EDUCATION LIMITED

Head Office:
Edinburgh Gate
Harlow CM20 2JE
Tel: +44 (0)1279 623623
Fax: +44 (0)1279 431059

London Office:
128 Long Acre, London WC2E 9AN
Tel: +44 (0)207 447 2000
Fax: +44 (0)207 240 5771
Website: www.business-minds.com

First published in Great Britain in 2001

© Pearson Education Limited 2001

The right of J. Brian Heywood to be identified as Author
of this Work has been asserted by him in accordance
with the Copyright, Designs and Patents Act 1988.

ISBN 0 273 65617 1

British Library Cataloguing in Publication Data
A CIP catalogue record for this book can be obtained from the British Library

10 9 8 7 6 5 4 3 2 1

Typeset by Pantek Arts Ltd, Maidstone, Kent
Printed and bound in Great Britain by Biddles of Guildford and King's Lynn.

The Publishers' policy is to use paper manufactured from sustainable forests.

about the author

● ●

My own involvement in the world of commerce began many years ago with a succession of roles in sales, market research, advertising and brand management. This experience eventually gained me a position as UK head of an American toiletries company. This was followed by a period of four years with a major management consultancy in the UK. I then spent four years based in the USA. During the last three of these years I was President of an American Food Company.

Since my return to the UK I have worked as an independent consultant largely to indulge my own and my family's desire to live on the south coast of England. During this period I also set up a marketing research company and have had a continuous involvement in this area. Some of my direct consultancy work has been via major consultancies and some has been done on an independent basis. Consequently, my 'clients' have ranged from the very large to the very small. Most of this consultancy work has been in areas related to marketing, business systems and in outsourcing. In recent years I have made a speciality of helping outsourcing service providers to find and get into new markets.

Amongst my successes I can claim technology research work that was used as the basis for futuristic television programmes around the world and a marketing award for helping small consultancy clients increase their sales. Amongst my failures are two attempts to set up manufacturing companies utilizing new technologies.

contents

● ● ● ● ● ● ● ● ● ● ● ● ● ●

introduction

● ● ● ● ● ● ● ● ● ● ● ● ● ● ● ● ● ● ●

Both the title of this book *The Outsourcing Dilemma* and the sub-title *The Search for Competitiveness* deal with the most frequently asked question in business today: 'How can we become competitive and remain competitive over all our business processes?' My conclusion is that outsourcing is probably the answer, but it is likely to be a different type of outsourcing from what is generally practised today.

Outsourcing is not something that can be considered in isolation. It has become a major factor in commerce because the dramatic advances in technology over the last few decades have created an almost intolerable situation for everybody involved in management. Managers in all organizations must now seek to achieve maximum competitiveness in performing all business processes. In order to do this, they must constantly evaluate the technology on offer and try to achieve performance improvements with what is usually a less than adequate internal skills base. Quite frequently, the need to bring about the desired change is both sudden and dictated by an external organization, for example, when supermarket chains began to demand that their suppliers utilized Electronic Data Interchange (EDI) systems. In these circumstances, the use of full-time external specialists through outsourcing has become an important solution to the problem of maintaining competitiveness.

However, outsourcing is just one possible solution to the competitiveness problem and any reasonable evaluation of the subject must logically compare it to other options that are being used or could be developed to enhance a competitive position. Most of these options have considerable merit even if they are not always equally applicable to all types and sizes of organization. However, whatever their merits and demerits, the truth is that all these theoretical solutions fail far too often in practice. I suggest, though, that the current failure rate of performance improvement projects is only tolerated because the full extent of failure is disguised; few organizations or individuals are willing to admit the extent of failure on a major project.

The vast majority of attempts to become more competitive can be divided into two parts: the internal solutions, which involve some type of performance improvement project, and the various external outsourcing options. All further references to internal projects in this book are to major projects that involve organizations in costly attempts to improve performance.

The results of a high technology project failure can be very damaging. The general public is constantly being reminded of the risks involved with high technology projects because they suffer as a result. In the UK, for example, the Department of Social Security has had a succession of computer disasters going back over many years, affecting many thousands of people and in 1999 50,000 people had their holiday plans disrupted when the Passport Agency's new project ran into trouble. Why is the consequence of failure not normally given adequate consideration prior to approving major projects? This is a particularly vexing question when one considers the number of research reports that have been published in recent times giving clues to senior managers regarding the potential for failure.

The main reason is, of course, that major projects are normally conceived to correct a current problem that is seen to be damaging the organization's competitive position and is likely to get worse. Consequently the senior management believe that the problem has to be corrected as soon as possible because the responsibility is clearly theirs. In such circumstances there is a certain amount of logic in the argument that goes: 'As the core problem had not been anticipated earlier we have no alternative but to carry out this project, so let's not dwell on the risk of failure, let's make sure it is a success'.

In a great many projects the senior management have a vested interest in not making the targets too difficult or the parameters for success too precise, because this will increase the chance of being seen to fail. Most senior managers will from time to time be faced with choosing between a project that is likely to provide the maximum benefit for the organization but will take a number of years before worthwhile results are seen, and another project that may be more expensive but will provide quicker results. As the tenure of office of senior managers gets shorter and shorter, it is only natural that managers increasingly look for short-term glory even though this may not be in the best interests of the organization. Centaur Application Software Services, the Aylesbury-based firm of management consultants, experienced this at first hand in 1995 when they carried out a series of direct selling calls on UK Finance Directors, warning of potential Y2K difficulties and offering a service to correct the problem. The consultancy was surprised by the number of FDs who openly made comments such as 'Five years is a long time off and it is likely to be someone else's problem then'.

A further indication of the declining tenure of office for senior managers came to light in late 1999 when the market research company TSS was asked to check certain marketing databases. Over a three month period earlier that year TSS called 600 of the 2000 largest organizations in the UK and established amongst other things, the name of the Finance Director. In one month late in the year they called all these organizations back again and found that during the six to nine month intervening period, just over 10 per cent of the organizations had obtained new Finance Directors.

Whatever the reasons, the risk of failure with major projects never seems to exercise the corporate mind to the extent it should. Only for a brief period did this subject get anywhere near the attention that it deserves. That was a few years ago when the American CSC Index for 1994 reported on a survey of 600 organizations and claimed that as many as 67 per cent of these companies reported zero or only marginally improved results from their business process re-engineering (BPR) projects. Even then, the concern was that BPR projects (which had previously been considered almost foolproof) could fail and not the fact that more projects had failed than had succeeded.

If, despite the natural internal desire to disguise failure, published reports can suggest that up to two thirds of projects fail – what must the true failure rate be?

We may never get an accurate reading for the number of project failures. Certainly, no amount of market research will settle this question. Apart from the problem of not being fully aware of the parameters and targets that are set for all the projects carried out, there is the question of how you measure success or failure when so few people are willing to admit the full extent of failure. All that the researchers who study these projects can normally claim is that failure rates are bound to be much worse than admitted.

At this point I must define what I mean by failure. These days any internal project begun with the objective of improving performance will be very likely to require considerable expenditure on new technology and external advice whilst also incurring the often difficult to quantify expense caused by disruption of normal activity. However, the real cost of such projects does not end there. A project to implement a new finance system, for example, can only be contemplated by most organizations once every five to seven years. Whatever the targets set, the logical minimum requirement from the project will be to put the service in question on a competitive basis immediately following the implementation and at the very least provide some hope for further improvements until a replacement project is put into action in the future. My definition of failure is reached by asking: 'Did the project achieve the minimum competitive requirements and was it still providing a competitive solution two years after implementation?' If it did not it is a failure and it remains a failure even if it was finished on time and to budget. It is a failure because the opportunity has been lost and it will be some time before the problem can be corrected. Conversely, I would rate the venture a potential success if it achieved the desired competitive performance levels but cost and time deadlines were narrowly missed.

My definition of a failed outsourcing project is also based on meeting the minimum competitiveness criteria. It used to be easy to spot the extreme outsourcing failures as these usually ended up in a courtroom, but many outsourcing contracts now contain provisions for dealing with disputes and therefore avoid the need to go to court. These special provisions will often stipulate the penalties the service provider must pay if the service fails to meet a certain standard. The trouble is that only on rare occasions will the outsourcing service provider have agreed to a minimum level of service that equates to competitiveness for the client.

In most outsourcing arrangements the service provider agrees a cost that is lower than the client is currently incurring but accepts a service target in excess of what the client is achieving. Having got such a deal, most client's eventually accept that the minimum service level should be set close to the client's own performance level, even though this may be far from competitive.

Given these circumstances, the service provider's staff will often convince themselves that they are doing a good job even though their performance only moves between the minimum service level and the targets set. Many outsourcing agreements go on like this year by year, with the service never quite falling to a level likely to cause a breach of the contract, but with the client nonetheless dissatisfied. But claims that more than a third of outsourcing contracts are never renewed, despite the cost of taking the service back or transferring it to another provider, give some clue about latent client dissatisfaction. As with internal projects, the real cost relates to the missed opportunity which cannot normally be corrected until the end of the contract.

An organization worried about its ability to bring about a performance improvement internally might well compare the limited experience and success it has previously enjoyed in this respect with the outsourcing specialist that carries out such projects on a frequent basis. From this point, it is a natural step to look for a service provider that can demonstrate success in the relevant area. However, this does not always guarantee a long and happy relationship. For example, CSL, the outsourcing division of Deloitte & Touche, had been very beneficial to the London Borough of Croydon when taking over its housing benefits system. Success in this area with this client led to CSL getting similar work for other local authorities. But in March 2000 the Chief Executive of CSL apologized for housing benefit disasters his organization were involved with at Sheffield City Council and a local authority in Somerset. There have also been problems between the London Borough of Islington and its housing benefits administration provider, ITNet. It would appear that at least part of the problem in this area of housing benefits has been repeated changes to the system by the government. However, many of the local authorities that kept this service in house have coped far better with these changes.

If both the internal and external options frequently fail, what can be done to resolve the performance improvement problem? Chief executives might be tempted to consider one of the alternative internal solutions that they have not yet tried. There are a number of alternative solutions in the form of management theories, with each new one appearing more radical than the previous one. Almost all make good sense and can be adopted completely if the circumstances are right. For example, 'Get rid of middle management'. It is certainly possible to find instances where organizations have benefited enormously from removing almost all middle management. Against that, many others now believe that even the modest reductions they made in middle management numbers has worsened rather than improved overall performance. This does not prove that it's right or wrong to get rid of middle managers – just that it may not be the ideal solution in all organizations at all times. Even where it does work, what do you do for an encore when you are asked to make further reductions to costs?

The call to 'Empower all employees to act like Chief Executive Officers' has also been widely promoted. Examples detailing success, however, largely concentrate on the benefits of letting widespread local service agents make most of their own decisions. It is difficult to see too many organizations introducing this concept completely in the average factory or in government offices and even more difficult to imagine how it would work. Perhaps the most radical of these proposed solutions can be found in the call to 'Forget change, it's time for revolution'. Again, the revolutionary or 'start again' approach to restructuring business functions has been responsible for some successes, but in the real world not every organization believes it can find a suitable time to begin a revolution.

Internal performance improvement projects are normally very expensive, time and resource consuming and prone to failure. Likewise outsourcing projects are also normally very expensive, time and resource consuming and prone to failure. The radical solutions will work for some, but most organizations would not even consider taking such steps on the grounds that their use would be inappropriate 'at this moment in time'.

Given these problems, it is necessary to ask: 'Is there a performance improvement answer "for the rest of us"?' Is there some way that the average organization can become competitive in its non-core functions, thereby improving overall competitiveness? Could we find an answer for the majority of organizations that goes further than the aims of the in-house, external and radical solutions discussed, i.e. one that enables the organization to remain competitive long after the change has been adopted? Web-enabling developments do offer some prospect for improvements in this area, but in addition, I believe that there is one simple solution that could be utilized by a significant number of organizations and it is explained in the last chapter of this book.

Back to the structure of the book. I have abbreviated the history of the subject matter and avoided detailed case histories because they tend to suggest that everything relating to the project concerned was a lasting success and this is not always the case.

The aim of this book is to present the arguments as fairly as possible and to suggest ways in which the monumental problem of maintaining competitiveness might be approached. In order to make the story flow, the main body of the book is confined to issues that need to be considered before taking a decision to outsource and most of the more technical 'how-to' outsource considerations are relegated to appendices.

Chapter 1 – deals with the changing times that have brought about the need to be competitive in all the functions and processes undertaken by organizations.

Chapter 2 – starts by asking the question 'How can you become competitive?' and then runs through the various internal solutions to the problem and questions the likelihood of success from pursuing these options.

Chapter 3 – introduces outsourcing, the external solution and probes the advantages and disadvantages of this option.

Chapter 4 – examines the extent to which outsourcing is currently being practised and the functions being outsourced.

Chapter 5 – looks at the growing range of alternatives to full outsourcing, including the various types of Shared Service Centres and the potential for ASP developments.

Chapter 6 – lists a range of factors that potential clients should know about outsourcing service providers and makes suggestions as to how to avoid some of the resulting problem areas.

Chapter 7 – outlines a number of factors to consider when choosing an outsourcing service provider.

Chapter 8 – details the potential benefits from outsourcing.

Chapter 9 – describes the real risks and concerns for both parties.

Chapter 10 – summarizes the alternative options towards achieving lasting competitiveness.

Chapter 11 – introduces 'Business Satellites', a long-term competitiveness option that does not require short-term dramatic change, expense and disruption. A number of theoretical Business Satellite ideas are developed to further illustrate how the concept might work.

Appendix A – a step-by-step procedure illustrating the various dos and don'ts for those client organizations interested in a conventional outsourcing arrangement.

Appendix B – actions necessary before the outsourcing transition gets underway.

Appendix C – a list of factors that should go into a conventional outsourcing contract.

Appendix D – the legal problem of transferring staff to an outsourcing service provider.

The relatively recent creation of the internet makes all current attempts at forecasting the commercial future hazardous, if not meaningless, because the potential for change cannot yet be fully understood. It is possible for example, that the current problems associated with major internal projects and outsourcing could be eased considerably by Web-enabling developments. At the time of writing there is great uncertainty about the potential for the application service provider (ASP) concept, which, in theory, would help to reduce software and other IT costs dramatically and make some types of outsourcing a more simple and acceptable concept. I am aware of some sizeable organizations that see the potential for Web-enabled software as an excuse to postpone projects until the situation becomes clearer. They may turn out to be right to delay, but the problem is not only the cost and availability of the technology but also finding enough suitably qualified people to deal with the technology, and that problem is not going to go away in the short or medium term.

If forecasting is difficult, it is probably also correct to say that no one is really qualified to successfully analyze what is currently happening in the world of commerce. It is all happening and changing too quickly for that to be possible. Nevertheless, I am certain of two facts: the first is that there is no one solution that is suitable for all types and sizes of organizations; and the second is that given the failure rate of current performance improvement projects, some long-term alternatives have to be found.

For what it is worth, my own involvement in the world of commerce began many years ago with a succession of roles in sales, market research, advertising and brand management. This experience eventually gained me a position as UK head of an American toiletries company. This was followed by a period of four years with a major management consultancy in the UK. I then spent four years based in the USA. During the last three of these years I was President of an American Food Company.

Since my return to the UK I have worked as an independent consultant largely to indulge my own and my family's desire to live on the south coast of England. During this period I also set up a marketing research company and have had a continuous involvement in this area. Some of my direct consultancy work has been via major consultancies and some has been done on an independent basis. Consequently, my 'clients' have ranged from the very large to the very small. Most of this consultancy work has been in areas related to marketing, business systems and in outsourcing. In recent years I have made a speciality of helping outsourcing service providers to find and get into new markets.

Amongst my successes I can claim technology research work that was used as the basis for futuristic television programmes around the world and a marketing award for helping small consultancy clients increase their sales. Amongst my failures are two attempts to set up manufacturing companies utilizing new technologies.

The title of this book *The Outsourcing Dilemma* deals with the most frequently asked question in business today: 'How can we become competitive and remain competitive over all our business processes?' My conclusion is that outsourcing is probably the answer but it is likely to be a different type of outsourcing than is generally practised today.

chapter 1

changing times in commerce

• • • • • • • • • • • • •

Introduction

In a famous eighteenth century children's story, a man called Rip Van Winkle went to bed one night and fell into a deep sleep that lasted for many years. The timeless appeal of the story is largely based on Rip's reaction to the changes he found when he awoke and the perceived overall effect of mankind's ingenuity on changing and 'improving' the way people live over time. When the story first appeared in print it was credited with forcing many people to think for the first time about changing lifestyles.

Although there have been few periods in human history when inventions and improved ways of working were not being created, it was clear well over a hundred years ago, that each new century produced disproportionately more developments than the preceding one and that this trend was likely to continue. It was also clear that every so often it became almost meaningless to keep looking for improvements in an area that had been made obsolete by a new invention. Therefore, once the gun had been invented it made more sense trying to produce a better gun than an improved sword.

The changes that traumatized the fictional Rip Van Winkle would, of course, be quite modest when compared to what we now all experience over just a few short years and we, of course, are only too aware that the rate of change is accelerating all the time. In fact the rate of change is now so marked that we sometimes fail to see that we are still trying to make the equivalent of an improved sword, when we should be looking in an entirely different direction.

Using the Rip Van Winkle theme, we can illustrate the accelerating rate of change in commerce by stating that a senior executive unfortunate enough to slip into a coma in 1945 would, on returning to full health 15 years later in 1960, have experienced relatively few business problems that were outside his understanding and experience. It is quite likely, therefore, that if he returned to his old job, he could have done so without finding too many surprises in terms of technological and procedural changes.

A similar unfortunate going into a coma in 1985 and attempting to return to work in 2000 would find a very different situation. He or she would have a much more difficult task adapting to the changes in technology and more importantly, the effect these changes have had on business practice.

However, having experienced the same business environment in 'snapshots' 15 years apart, the year 2000 returner would probably see one problem, currently considered by many to be 'almost beyond solution', much more clearly than those of us who worked the key problem facing management at the start of this century – the need to be competitive in all the various functions of business – appeared to be far less important in 1985

through this period. This is so because the key problem facing management at the start of this century – the need to be competitive in all the various functions of business– appeared to be far less important in 1985. Consequently, the current emphasis on competitiveness would be very marked to anyone who missed the years in between.

• •

What is so different about competitiveness now?

Until the last decade or so of the last century, established organizations usually had sufficient time to adjust to all but the most catastrophic changes in business circumstances. If, for example, a company's sales increased or decreased unexpectedly, the change invariably took place at a rate that was, in corporate terms, easily controllable and not usually seen as a reason for undue concern. In many cases it was just a matter of adjusting the number of employees and the long established organizations built up considerable expertise in handling problems of this type. Having made the necessary corrections, it was normal to expect that no further change would be necessary to that area for at least a year or so.

Fundamental to this expertise was the creation of business structures or functions that developed according to the type of organization, i.e. public sector organizations would be mainly broken down into administrative functions and manufacturing concerns would be split into manufacturing, finance, sales, etc. In each organization the various functions would come under the control of senior managers who were specialists in their respective areas. In this way the various business activities or processes were grouped together to make them easier to manage. One effect of grouping these processes into distinct functions was the creation of hierarchies, which in turn often produced layers of middle management in the functions.

During the early to middle part of the century, a certain 'sameness' developed in organizations in similar business areas and industries. For example, up until the 1970s, food manufacturers tended to have the same functional areas and structure within functions, irrespective of size or country of manufacture. In effect, business 'norms' had been created by which the senior managers could, to some extent, judge their own performance. By and large this came about because senior executives tended to look for jobs within the sector they understood and employers almost always believed that knowledge of their sector was essential, even when they were recruiting for non-core functions. For most of the century this was senior management's main guide as to how the various functions should be constructed. Having developed in this way, the functions would frequently operate as independent units between which there was sometimes only occasional contact.

Only on very rare occasions did anyone seriously challenge this type of structure. Those that did were mainly academics and their arguments largely failed because they could not come up with suitable alternatives. The perceived business wisdom, therefore, was that an ideal method of managing an organization had developed over many years and it had been tried and tested – so it had to be right. Given these circumstances it was normal for changes to be made to one function in isolation from other parts of the organization. Even when management consultants were brought in to try to improve performance they often looked for savings from the relevant function without considering the full impact elsewhere in the organization. Organizations were thus guilty of looking in on themselves and to some extent ignoring the accelerating change that was affecting their marketplace and individual customers.

During the 1990s all this began to change. The competitive pressure became so strong that the continued existence of everything and everyone in business was soon being challenged. Technology developments changed some processes, made others obsolete and effectively moved some from one function to another, e.g. from finance to IT. The management theorists began to argue that the time had come to knock down the hierarchical walls and create a flatter, more competitive management structure by getting rid of middle management. Over the last few years management structures have got notably flatter in many organizations, with many of the redundant middle managers being used in new, often technical specialist, roles that reflect the organizations' changing circumstances.

Heads of functions dealing with these changes were therefore under pressure from an unprecedented number of directions. Apart from the usual problems of maintaining the quality of their service, they had to contend with the threat to their empires and cope with naturally concerned subordinates.

A number of factors were responsible for creating this situation. These included the globalization of commerce, benchmarking, dramatically improved communications, as well as a range of other technology developments, which frequently emerged as packaged software.

Taken all together, these changes and threats add up to one conclusion – in future each manager's main responsibility is to achieve and maintain the competitiveness of the processes that are under his or her control. Obviously, competitive pressure has always existed for the majority of organizations but in the 1990s it took on a new momentum and meaning, simply because its importance was becoming more obvious.

> in future each manager's main responsibility is to achieve and maintain the competitiveness of the processes that are under his or her control

The importance of the competitive issue is illustrated by the fact that a significant proportion of the articles and books currently being printed on business subjects, concentrate in some way or other, on the problem of how to be competitive and remain competitive.

We must now accept that there is both a threat and an opportunity continuously present in every function in every organization. Manage the function well and you have a competitive advantage; manage it badly and you will be in trouble. If you performed the function badly in the 1990s you were more likely to suffer than if you did so in the 1980s and if you do it badly in the first few years of the new millennium, then your corporate house is going to come under pressure that much quicker.

All procedures and processes must now be analyzed continuously and, ideally, collectively. It is no longer possible to concentrate on a few 'key' tasks and leave the others to look after themselves. It is now rarely correct to look at performance levels of functions in isolation. Each function is part of a body that is being continuously pushed and pulled by increasingly strong competitive forces and you need to know the direction the body is going in to justify any significant change.

With this in mind it is interesting to compare the PR handouts issued by the major management consultancies over the years. In the 1980s a typical claim would illustrate what the consultancy had achieved in function X for client Y. Now consultancies like Booz-Allen & Hamilton appear to limit their PR case histories to where they have worked with the client across all its functions on a single project.

For many organizations, the internet has only just started to influence the competitive situation but few can be in any doubt that it will make the situation more rather than less difficult to control. The net result of all of this is that you cannot be sure that the savings and improvements you made this month will be sufficient to keep you competitive next month.

• • • • • • • • • • • • • • • •

Benchmarking

In addition to all their other worries, the functional heads have to consider that the development of benchmarking techniques, in theory at least, now provide their chief executives with a good guide to the relative performance of each function.

> benchmarking has become one of those concepts that can influence an organization even where it is not being practised internally

In recent years, the concept of 'benchmarking' has grown in importance without ever being as widely used as it could be. Benchmarking has become one of those concepts that can influence an organization even where it is not being practised internally. For example, the publication of a report a number of years back showing that it cost one American meat packing plant 25 cents to produce an invoice, quite naturally caused concern to directly competitive finance directors, some of whom had an invoicing cost up to 12 times as large. More surprisingly, perhaps, the same report was mulled over by very different organizations, including manufacturing and financial services groups, all over the world. Simply knowing that such a wide disparity could exist in an industry that was made up of simple, apparently easily controllable 'manufacturing' processes, caused executives to look more closely at their own situation.

Gradually, an increasing number of such benchmarking reports put pressure on functional heads all over the world, as chief executives sought to explain ever increasing costs. Even where attempts at benchmarking have been badly thought out, or failed for other reasons, the concept has been fully accepted. The key fact in all of this is that benchmarking techniques will continue to improve and gradually functional heads in even quite small organizations will know what is achievable for an organization of their type and size, in terms of costs and service levels. The internet-based Benchnet organization claims over 2500 member organizations in 50 countries and it is apparent that new members offering benchmarking services across a wide range of functions are joining Benchnet every day.

Clearly all heads of functions now have to consider the question of competitiveness much more seriously than their counterparts in 1985. The key question is: what can they do about it?

chapter 2

how can an organization become and stay competitive?

Although some of them were loath to accept it, the governments of virtually every country in the world now acknowledge that they cannot create wealth for their citizens – that has to be done by the business community and in particular the entrepreneurs. The importance of being competitive is nevertheless recognized by most governments and many of them now attempt to provide direct help and advice on the subject for their business communities.

In some countries entrepreneurs can still base their schemes on the availability of raw materials and or cheap labour. Given such circumstances the entrepreneur may not initially need to put too much emphasis on controlling costs and improving service.

In most of the developed world, however, any competitive edge must be found via knowledge, skills and creativity improvements. Sadly, not all these benefits continue over the long term, because modern technology has a habit of distributing most of the knowledge and skills developments around the competition, quite quickly.

In the period following World War II, the solution to the competitiveness problem appeared to many people to be quite straightforward. They argued that organizations had to keep extending their customer base until they were operating in as wide an international arena as possible. Continuous expansion in this way met the pressure of competition by spreading costs and revenue on a global scale. Many large corporations have achieved an ongoing competitiveness by deliberately positioning themselves on a global basis. Nevertheless, it is not a solution that all organizations can aspire to and it can only be a part solution to the giants of commerce because eventually they must run out of new territory to conquer. Coca-Cola has a global image but can never relax its efforts because Pepsi and other competitors have also obtained a global or near global status.

Competitiveness will normally involve some mixture of quality, continuous service improvement, speed of performance and cost reduction. The exact mix will depend upon the nature of the organization. Globalization by itself can therefore never be a complete answer even for the larger organizations. For every organization that has attempted to solve the competitive problem by globalization there must be hundreds who just rely on cutting costs. Organizations that lurch from one cost-cutting exercise to another are usually hoping that if they keep reducing costs then eventually they will gain access to a creative breakthrough that solves their problem.

> competitiveness will normally involve some mixture of quality, continuous service improvement, speed of performance and cost reduction

The trouble with this line of reasoning is that real creative breakthroughs, although happening faster than ever before, are not a daily occurrence. For most of the time, therefore, executives who are constantly under pressure to make 'savings' can only contribute to the competitive situation by looking for cost reductions and consequently spend less than the necessary time on much needed service improvements. Such savings are frequently made from within a function and without knowledge of the situation facing the entire organization. As a result this action may, in some circumstances, be counter-productive.

To return to the question raised at the beginning of this chapter – how can an organization find or create the resources necessary to be competitive in everything it does? The important second part of this question is: If an organization manages to achieve a suitably improved level of performance in all functions, how long would it be reasonable to expect all of these functions to remain competitive?

Methods normally taken to improve performance

Although there are no golden or set rules to determine what management can or cannot do to improve performance, the following three elements account for most of the effort currently made when an internal solution is sought. Increasingly, for major organizations, at least, all three are brought together in one project.

- The use of management techniques

- Implementing packaged systems and other technology

- Using management consultants.

Management techniques developed to improve performance

In recent times, a plethora of management tools, techniques, ideas and methodologies, such as value engineering, change management, best practice and business process re-engineering (BPR) have been developed to assist executives to achieve a strong competitive situation.

Perhaps the most successful and widely promoted management technique of the last decade has been BPR, devised by Mike Hammer and James Champy. Whereas techniques such as total quality management (TQM) concentrate on improving existing processes, BPR requires the organization to rethink and redesign the process to bring it into line with customer needs. A successful BPR exercise will involve a number of distinct steps, starting with identifying the customer needs and ending with the redesign and implementation of the new process.

Some dramatic improvements in performance (15 to 50 per cent) have been claimed for successful BPR exercises. Against that it is sometimes reported that BPR projects fail more often than they succeed.

It goes without saying that all the management techniques have merit and will have benefited some of the organizations that have used them. It is equally possible that the vast majority of organizations would have obtained real benefit if the projects had been designed or carried out correctly.

Why should a technique that is so successful for some organizations fail when it is applied to others? Lack of or poor specialist advice is frequently blamed, but the ultimate responsibility for failure must lie with senior management. Senior management must take responsibility for performance improvement projects. In doing so they must understand what is required to bring about successful change and empower the project leader to bring about or recommend all the changes necessary. In addition they must be prepared to pass up the chance of limited short-term success if the best interests of the organization are best suited by a more long-term approach.

Questions *Has your performance reached truly competitive levels from using one of these techniques?*

Do you think that utilizing one of these techniques will enable you to achieve and maintain a competitive standard?

The packaged software solution to performance problems

In both North America and Europe, a few major companies are still using bespoke systems that were first installed in the 1970s or even earlier and have been added to and updated ever since. Most organizations, however, prefer to buy packaged solutions to control their main business functions. For them any significant improvements in the packaged systems available are welcome if their availability coincides with a previously perceived need to change systems, and unwelcome if what is now accepted as an inferior system has just been implemented.

In the late 1970s the software vendors and consultancies dealing in financial systems software often described their product as 'good for five years in present form', and in addition promised regular updates. In practice, a significant number of organizations bought new software from other vendors well within five years, but hoped that this time they would not be called upon to go through the considerable expense and upheaval of a further implementation in the near future. Almost invariably they were again forced to implement new systems from a different vendor well before the anticipated life of the system was exhausted or struggle on with a system that was no longer competitive. Typically, the reasons given for further changes were as follows.

● The promised benefits from the existing system were never obtained.

● Our business is changing and the existing system cannot meet our future needs.

● It would cost too much to modernize the existing system.

● Better systems have become available recently which will enable us to provide a more competitive service.

> most organizations seriously underestimate the cost of implementing new systems by making 'working life' assumptions that are never normally

Experience shows that most organizations seriously underestimate the cost of implementing new systems by making 'working life' assumptions that are never normally achieved.

The cost and disruption caused by such change is therefore increasing. The need to change major systems and the fear of failure is the key reason why organizations begin to consider outsourcing functions like finance.

Over the last few years of the 1990s the implementation of Enterprise Resource Planning (ERP) systems has been promoted as a major solution to keeping process costs low and the service at a competitive standard. However, most organizations struggled to find the right quality of staff when they implemented specialist 'best of breed' financial and manufacturing systems. Why should the situation be improved when organizations implement even more complicated integrated systems?

Unfortunately, the need to change systems now appears to be happening more frequently, with some organizations having switched from one ERP supplier to another within three years of completing the first ERP implementation.

Confidence in this type of solution was still high in early 2000, but in mid to late 2000 negative publicity began to appear at an increasing rate. For example, PA Consulting reported that 92 per cent of organizations in a research exercise they had carried out, admitted that their ERP project (some of which had taken four years to implement) had failed to meet the targets set.

These failures have been explained by assuming that the main problem is due to the fact that project teams were attempting to do something they had never tried before and comparisons are being made, for the same reason, with the high failure rate of Data Warehousing projects. Senior management groups are nonetheless being advised that other new concepts, such as Customer Relationship Management (CRM), are more likely to succeed.

I believe that on a worldwide basis, the majority of large IT projects have always failed to reach their full potential by a significant margin and that this situation is very likely to continue.

Surely, the real problem stems from the fact that the ultimate aim is often difficult to set out. This is mainly due to not knowing what the competitive requirement is likely to be at various stages in the future and the ineptitude and short-term nature of management thinking. However, the ever increasing implementation periods and shortage of suitable skills also plays a major part.

Building a bridge over a major river will seem to most people like a very daunting task but in many ways it is considerably more straightforward than a typical large scale IT project. In bridge building you know where the opposite shore is and you know that you will have to build in a straight line towards it. In IT projects the opposite shoreline is often only a faint image and often keeps moving. Then instead of engineers the skill shortage often means you have to make do with the equivalent of bricklayers. In the circumstances it is not surprising that the IT version of bridge building often produces sections going in the wrong direction.

Questions *Have you got pleasant memories of implementing the last major system?*

Do you welcome the thought of doing it all again?

Do you know the cost, including consultancy, preparing invitations to tender (ITTs), installation and implementation of the last project?

Was the cost justified by improved performance?

Do you think changing the systems will enable the functions affected to become competitive?

Do you think a new system will justify the cost in performance and competitive terms?

How long do you think the new system will enable you to remain competitive?

Using management consultants

Organizations are using management consultants at a greater rate than ever before. For the larger established consultancies, at least, the late 1990s represented a period of almost

organizations are
using management
consultants at a
greater rate than
ever before

continuous boom. Admittedly, work that was directly related to Y2K problems tended to fall away in the latter half of 1999, but all the indications are that the consultancy train has started to pick up speed again.

The vast majority of consultancy assignments have always concentrated on trying to improve a client's performance in a function or group of functions. However, there has been a fundamental change over the years in the way that consultants carry out their work.

Prior to the late 1970s most consultants carried out what is often now referred to as theoretical consulting. Depending to a large extent on the function under investigation, the consultant would concentrate on understanding what was required of the service and then produce a report outlining new and hopefully better ways of doing the work. With theoretical consulting the emphasis was on the report and the client was left alone to carry out the practical effort necessary to bring about the change. The consultant was therefore rarely in a position where blame or criticism was likely to stick.

These days most consultancy assignments are of a practical nature. The consultant is engaged to provide specialist advice and then work with the client's staff to make the necessary changes.

The gradual movement in emphasis from theoretical to practical consultancy was triggered by technology developments. Practical consultancy would have been possible without these developments but, in the event, technology provided the spur. The extent of the change towards practical consulting can be judged from the fact that many of the large consultancies derived from an auditing base now describe themselves in terms that emphasize the practical systems development nature of their services.

Consultants are bound to be better advisers if they have past experience of implementing change and, in practical consulting, they are forced to accept responsibility for their ideas. This means there can be few clients who would prefer to employ consultants on a theoretical basis.

Nevertheless, there was one advantage in theoretical consultancy that to a large degree has been lost. A consultant asked to study a business or a function of a business prior to the mid 1970s, did so without the pressure of ready-made software solutions piling up daily in front of the team members. Often the theoretical consultant was the only person ever to have both the time and inclination to look for an ideal solution since the organization was founded. Frequently, the consultant had no idea what the solution was until the 'main findings' were finally submitted to paper after which the answer often became beautifully obvious. The key point here is that the old style consultant could not trust the client's staff to give an accurate analysis of what was required from any given process and was therefore forced to get the answer from 'the customer'. Now many assignments start with client and consultant studying the range of ready-made package solutions and consequently many projects end up concentrating on improving the current service and neglecting to ask if it is the right service. Such shortcuts are difficult to justify at a time when so much emphasis is being placed on understanding customer needs.

> such shortcuts are difficult to justify at a time when so much emphasis is being placed on understanding customer needs

Clearly, BPR and techniques like strategy consulting ought to provide the opportunity to discover what is required of the function. Management consultants might justifiably claim that they would always try to establish the customer needs for the foreseeable future if they are given the time and the opportunity. On too many occasions, however, the consultants start an assignment by accepting the client's short-list of alternative options.

No one can doubt that the standard of management consultancy has improved continuously over the years, but the number of really satisfied clients does not appear to have increased at the same rate. Is it possible, that at a time when continuous improvement is essential, management consultants fail their clients because they are not active on the client's behalf on a continuous basis? Despite the practical help they provide, could it sometimes be dangerous to use such specialists on an irregular basis when the competitive marketplace is changing so quickly?

Questions *Do you believe that employing management consultants in your own organization will enable you to become competitive and remain competitive for any length of time?*

Have you achieved significantly improved performance levels from using management consultants in the past?

How effective are performance improvement projects?

There cannot be many sizeable organizations that have not subjected some, at least, of their core and non-core functions to a range of cost-cutting and performance improvement projects over the last 15 years or so. In many cases, two or all three of the elements described above – management techniques, packaged systems, management consultants – will have been part of the project mix. Certainly, very few projects are completed without dipping into scarce resources to purchase the latest hardware and software technology available or in fashion.

It is impossible to know how many such projects the originating project sponsor considered successful and in any case, that will depend, to some extent, on the targets that were originally set and how long the technology chosen remained desirable. Anybody studying a large sample of CVs submitted by project managers would naturally surmise that all projects are successful and delivered on time and to budget. On the other hand, the reports of research companies that check out after implementation projects using packaged software, would suggest that results don't often match expectations.

It may be that some managers are badly advised, fail to adequately manage the project, or just don't understand what is involved. In many cases, however, a failure to improve performance after one of these projects can be directly attributed to a desire to avoid the trauma of major change and the resulting redundancies. Too often the failures are associated with management reluctance to make difficult decisions. In other words the parameters necessary to obtain the desired results were either fudged or ignored.

This problem was illustrated very well during the 1970s craze for centralizing and decentralizing. Almost every time a highly decentralised organization approached a management consultancy and asked 'Would we make savings by centralizing?' the consultancy proved that it could. However, almost every time a highly centralized organization asked if savings were possible from decentralizing, the result again turned out to be positive. Management consultancies took a lot of criticism for their role in this matter but much of it was unjustified. Usually the client organizations were well aware that the savings were resulting from releasing people and processes that were no longer essential to running the business, and that they would not have always achieved such savings if major relocation issues were not present to provide an excuse.

Clearly, in a rapidly changing business world the needs of customers must be constantly changing. Why then should anyone assume that the way the function or process was carried out in, say, 1970 is necessarily still the right way. Obviously, every responsible manager will accept this need to adapt, but apparently a significant number of them do so 'half heartedly'. This was apparent in the 1970s when the centralize/decentralize saga was in progress and it is clearly still happening today.

Whatever the causes, it is generally accepted that projects fail too often to meet a reasonable amount of the targets set for them. For a number of reasons it will always be difficult to label projects as simply successes or failures. For one thing, the parameters for judging success and failure are rarely adequately laid down prior to the commencement of projects, and for another it is not easy admitting that you have been associated with a failure. However, questions aimed at project sponsors such as 'With hindsight, if you had to do it again, what changes would you make?' almost always produce responses that suggest at least a degree of failure.

Questions *How many of the projects that you have been involved with were deemed successful?*

If the minimum requirement is to reduce costs by 20–30 per cent, improve the service and then bring about further savings and improvements in subsequent years – how many of your projects would be considered successful?

Are you just tinkering with the systems?

When dealing with the problem of competitiveness, all the people writing and lecturing on the subject appear to agree on one fact. In a time of accelerating change, they argue, it is no good tinkering with existing systems and structures. As the rate of change is likely to increase, the universally held view now is that any organization seeking to become competitive must re-think or re-engineer each business process from scratch.

> the universally held view now is that any organization seeking to become competitive must re-think or re-engineer each business process from scratch

There are considerable advantages in starting an organization from scratch. When in 1945 the allies assisted West Germany to rebuild its industries, they took many steps that enabled that country to achieve considerable competitive advantage. The British Trade Union movement played its part in creating West Germany's extraordinary revival by helping to set up a system that effectively resulted in only one union operating in each factory. In this way the West German industry had a sensible union structure which helped to reduce the number of days lost to strikes and disruptions. By comparison, in the decades following World War II, British industry was at a considerable disadvantage from 'demarcation' and other disputes that were exacerbated by having multiples of unions operating in the same workplace.

Why did the British Trade Union movement not adopt the policy it recommended to West Germany? The obvious answer is that the British union bosses had their empires to protect. Why does management often fail to take difficult decisions during performance improvement projects? Clearly the protection of empires is a major factor.

Starting from scratch is easy if your organization is virtually destroyed by war and reasonably straightforward if a major relocation or reorganization due to acquisitions or mergers is involved. Otherwise it seems most managers are not mentally strong enough or far sighted enough to carry out the changes necessary to put their organizations on a truly competitive footing. It is certainly true to say that fear of failure and other reasons have prevented many managers aiming for targets that they might reasonably have been expected to achieve.

. . . .

Becoming 'world class'

Many writers on management issues argue that for a business to grow significantly, it you must aspire to become 'world class'. But to succeed in this way it has to achieve world class status in most of the processes it carries out in the normal course of business.

Here lies one of the major problems in trying to remain competitive in the twenty-first century. For non-core functions such as IT and finance to remain competitive in most business situations, costs will need to be reduced and service improved on a regular basis. For most organizations this will mean, at the very best, fewer key roles for the relevant executives. In turn this is likely to mean that the really capable executives will seek employers that can offer growth in their specialist area.

So how can an organization remain competitive in all or most of its functions or business processes? Regular re-engineering will probably be out of the question, when considering the management time involved. Admittedly, the redesign stage of BPR can be completed in just a few days when done for a second or third time, but new implementations often take as long as the original. In any case, it is unlikely that any amount of re-engineering will transfer non-core functions into the sort of departments that will attract the best people.

Questions	*Are you sure that you are not trying to improve the sword, when your competitors are currently using tanks and working on the development of laser guided weapons?*

Why assume that competitors will obtain ongoing world class status?

At this stage, this is a very fair question. A reasonable summary of the statements made so far in Chapter 2, might be as follows.

● There will continue to be developments in technology, probably at a gradually increasing rate.

● From now on all heads of functions will need to ensure that their performance levels are maintained at a level that keeps them competitive. This means that the service provided must be continually improved and the costs stabilized or reduced.

- Benchmarking and, perhaps, other techniques will be developed to highlight good and poor performances within months of them occurring.

- A range of management techniques, software systems and consultants with their methodologies are on hand to provide salvation.

- Sadly, a significant number of projects set up to achieve this salvation fail to meet the main targets set for them. Failure can result from a variety of reasons, but quite often it happens because management backs away from taking difficult decisions. There is no sign that management is improving in this respect.

- Even where a project has been successful, it does not mean that the improvement or newly found competitiveness will automatically last for a significant amount of time.

It would be difficult to argue with the above summary but some managers studying it might nevertheless come to the following conclusions.

- 'A negative benchmarking report would be damaging, but there is only so much I can do to change and improve the existing structure.'

- 'If so many performance improvement projects fail, why should I assume that any of our competitors are going to achieve this, so called, world class?'

- 'Even if a competitor should achieve world class status, how long will they be able to keep it?'

- 'Why should we be concerned by these developments?'

· ·

The reason for concern

The reason why managers must now strive to be competitive in everything is quite simple. In recent times it has been proved that if the circumstances are right, it is possible to obtain substantial service improvements and cost savings from both core and non-core functions by involving external specialists on a continuous basis. Furthermore, it is possible to take action that will enable an organization to obtain even greater improvements and savings in the years ahead whilst passing much of the worry and responsibility to a third party.

In June 1995 an article appeared in the *Harvard Business Review* in which the Head of IT at BP Exploration claimed that by outsourcing almost all his IT function to

> it is possible to obtain substantial service improvements and cost savings from both core and non-core functions by involving external specialists on a continuous basis

specialist IT companies, he had achieved considerable benefits. Amongst the benefits claimed was a much improved service, a 30–40 per cent reduction in costs and a guarantee of further improvements and savings in the future. Later the Finance Director of BP Exploration went into print to say that he had just completed a four year contract for the outsourcing of his finance function and had signed a further five year contract with the same service provider. He went on to say that over the nine years of the two contracts, BP Explorations business will have grown by 50 per cent, although his costs will have reduced by 50 per cent and yet he now has a far better service.

Ever since the 1989 decision by Eastman Kodak to outsource most of its IT operations there has been a gradual increase in articles and PR releases which appear to indicate that a level of service improvements and cost savings might be possible from outsourcing that would be very difficult to obtain from an internal service. The BP Exploration articles added further weight to the outsourcing argument by suggesting that continuous improvements to the service were also a realistic target for some client organizations. After the first of these articles, there was a very noticeable decline in the number of managers claiming that outsourcing a function like IT was simply an admission of failure.

Certainly, BP Exploration's competitors were left in no doubt that to get back on a competitive footing regarding IT and finance, they had to look for equally innovative solutions. Recently, a number of these competitors have done just that. In most cases the dominant factor has been the involvement of external specialists in both IT and finance.

Apart from BP Exploration there are many other examples of both client and service provider jointly claiming dramatic success from an outsourcing arrangement. The logic of outsourcing a non-core function to an external specialist in a relevant field has to be theoretically sound. Why should an organization insist on employing the members of its non-core finance function when it has long ago outsourced functions like Security, Catering and Cleaning and would no longer even consider taking them back inhouse?

Given its proven potential, it is now clearly illogical to embark on a major performance improvement project without including outsourcing as one of the main options. The prospect that competitors could achieve continuous improvements and savings by taking such action is perhaps the key cause for concern when considering the entire subject of competitiveness. Clearly, not all the competition will take the action necessary to maximize competitiveness but most organizations would be in difficulty even if only a small percentage of their competitors obtained such an advantage.

But does this mean that all organizations should outsource their non-core functions? Are dramatic savings and service improvements open to all? Is outsourcing always the answer?

The short answer to this last question is No! Outsourcing does not always work, in fact there are many examples of abject failure. Indeed, the failure rate may be even greater than is normally experienced for internal projects. Nevertheless, the potential rewards are such that failure to consider the outsourcing option is no longer just a management misdemeanour, it's a very serious crime. Consider this: if you succeed with an internal project, how long will it be before a further project will be necessary – six months, a year or two years? If you successfully outsource to a provider who is motivated and skilful enough to make continuous improvements, then you will have to be careful in managing the relationship, but you can do so in the knowledge that the very best efforts are being made on your behalf for many years ahead.

Contrary to one common theory, outsourcing is not just something that only major prestigious organizations can benefit from. Many major client organizations have been very unsuccessful in their efforts to outsource, whereas some small organizations with as few as five employees have been very successful in outsourcing functions.

> contrary to one common theory, outsourcing is not just something that only major prestigious organizations can benefit from

It is distinctly possible for most client organizations, large and small, to gain great benefit from outsourcing at least some of their non-core functions. In order to do so they will need to work hard at understanding what is possible and it may be necessary for them to seek out or create the ideal providers.

In order to understand how this could be done and to illustrate why some deals succeed and some fail, it is necessary to examine the various issues, trends, successes, risks and failures taking place in the market. This is attempted in the following chapters.

chapter **3**

● ● ● ● ● ● ● ● ● ● ● ● ● ● ● ● ●

the outsourcing alternative

Outsourcing defined

The most complete definition of the outsourcing concept that I know of is:

'... the transferring of an internal business function or functions, plus any associated assets, to an external supplier or service provider who offers a defined service for a specified period of time, at an agreed but probably qualified price'.

It must be understood that the *control* of the functions in question will thus reside with the service provider. This outside organization, as a specialist in its field, will usually be in a position to add value not normally obtainable in a non-core function retained in house.

outsourcing has now become a familiar idea to the business and associated media world

Outsourcing has now become a familiar idea to the business and associated media world. However, it is often used as an umbrella term for a variety of different arrangements, not all of which involve adding value or the permanent transfer of personnel. These arrangements may be better defined by the following terms.

Outsourcing terms

Facilities management

The term 'facilities management' (FM) is sometimes used interchangeably with the term 'outsourcing'. However, whereas outsourcing is associated with adding value, an FM agreement simply transfers responsibility for the management of existing staff, property and equipment. For example, where an organization wishes to transfer just that part of its IT function that deals with established or legacy systems, including all staff, hardware, systems software and communications involved in the day-to-day running of the function, a conventional FM agreement should suffice. However, if it also wishes to transfer the development of applications systems and the applications staff, then it would be more correct to describe the arrangement as an outsourcing agreement, because it would include an element of added value.

Full or total outsourcing

This term is used to indicate that the staff and, possibly, assets relating to the whole of a major business area (in practice about 90 per cent of it), such as IT or finance, will be transferred to the service provider for the period of the contract.

Part or selective outsourcing

Under this sort of agreement, a significant part of the function will be retained in house.

Co-sourcing

Co-sourcing was originally devised by EDS to describe its own version of partnership outsourcing. In recent times, however, some people have used the term to describe outsourcing arrangements involving multiple providers.

Transitional outsourcing

This occurs when an organization transfers control of its legacy systems/platforms to a third party in the belief that its own internal IT staff have the abilities necessary for the development of new systems. Any organization becoming involved in transitional outsourcing would be demonstrating an unusually high level of confidence in the development capabilities of internal IT staff.

Transformational outsourcing

In the opposite of transitional outsourcing, an organization brings in a service provider to completely re-engineer the work of the function, probably developing new systems and building up a reliable skill base for the client to take over. Transformational outsourcing differs from full outsourcing only in that the transfer of people and assets is not permanent – at the end of the project the client regains full control and responsibility. To many people this sounds like a straight consultancy assignment. The difference is that in transformational outsourcing the provider normally works quite independently from the client's staff. Not surprisingly, perhaps, there are few real examples of transformational outsourcing.

Joint venture outsourcing

A joint venture agreement involves setting up a new company to exploit a perceived business opportunity. The client's staff and assets will then be transferred to this joint venture company, rather than to the service provider. The aim will be not only to improve the transferred service but also and, perhaps, more importantly, to develop products and services that can be sold to third parties. Client and service provider will then share the profits from the new company. Thus the service provider can fully exploit its systems development potential, with the client sharing the development costs of new software products. At the same time, the joint venture benefits from the client's specialized knowledge of their marketplace. Some joint venture products and services have been developed over time from opportunities that have arisen out of full outsourcing arrangements already in place.

Equity stakes

Some outsourcing relationships have been strengthened by either the client or the provider taking an equity stake in the other. Where it is the provider taking this step, it may be seen as a demonstration of their commitment to the best interests of their client. Where it is the client taking the equity stake in the provider on the other hand, it is often seen as a form of security. This was the assumption made by the outsourcing market at large when Swiss Bank signed an outsourcing deal with a provider, Perot Systems, taking a 24 per cent stake in Perot. However, the deal also demonstrated that the bank must have been impressed by

> some outsourcing relationships have been strengthened by either the client or the provider taking an equity stake in the other

what Perot had to offer. A similar event occurred in September 1997 when the Commonwealth Bank and EDS Australia signed what was then claimed to be the world's largest financial services outsourcing IT contract. The deal was worth $5 billion over ten years and involved the Commonwealth Bank taking a $240 million, 35 per cent share in EDS Australia.

● ●

The development of outsourcing

In the 1990s, some management theorists argued that the important factor in maintaining competitiveness was differentiating between core and non-core functions and then transferring all non-core functions to a specialist in that function. This was not a particularly new idea but it was certainly one 'whose time had come'. As discussions on the subject increased and evolved, the concept of the virtual organization was born. The theory behind the virtual organization is that any function that is not core should be transferred to an external specialist in that function. In addition, however, it argues that there are bound

> the theory behind the virtual organization is that any function that is not core should be transferred to an external specialist in that function

to be organizations that will perform your core functions better than you do – so why not transfer those as well? A number of organizations have recently been created on this principle, i.e. all, or almost all, the functions have been outsourced from day one – leaving behind only the 'soul' of the business. It is too soon to come to any conclusion as to the rights and wrongs of starting an enterprise this way. Nevertheless, it will be interesting to see what happens to them over the medium and long term.

It is now generally accepted that however a function or group of business processes is structured or managed, improvements done on a one-off basis are, at best, fire-fighting exercises. The ideal solution would involve putting each individual function or group of processes in a position where it is able to take up new technology developments when they first appear and to seek out continuous improvements, in order to remain competitive.

It is possible to lay down the necessary requirements for the function head to be able to achieve this aim.

- The function should, ideally, be core.

- The function should be capable of continuous growth in order to attract the best quality workers.

- The function should be in a position to grow by taking on additional clients.

There is a strong argument for saying that if management cannot make a case for the continuous growth of a function then they should strongly consider one or more of the externalization options.

The virtual organization concept may be very new, but externalizing functions to outside specialists has been practised for many years under various names: contract manufacturing, facilities management, outsourcing and insourcing. For example, many major firms of accountants will freely admit that even at the beginning of the twentieth century they had clients for whom they did the 'books' rather than the audit, and this situation remains true today.

With hindsight 'externalizing' might have been a better name than 'outsourcing' to describe the range of business activities that have grown up on the basic business idea that if your organization does not specialize in a particular function, then it will probably be beneficial in terms of cost and quality of service to transfer the control of the function to a specialist organization.

Contract manufacturers and people involved in the facilities management business will generally agree that they are in an outsourcing business. However, when most people hear or see the word outsourcing they normally think of IT outsourcing.

The outsourcing of IT functions started to happen on a major scale because of the high cost of processing power in the 1970s. This situation forced even major organizations to get at least some of their computer solutions from computer bureaux. The realization that the enormous expense that they might only recently have incurred on hardware was not going to keep them competitive for very long was a defining factor in the move towards outsourcing.

Knowing that they had to maintain existing systems, yet invest further in the hardware, software and specialists necessary to move into expensive replacement systems concentrated the corporate mind. Senior management began to worry that their IT departments were taking an ever increasing share of time and resources and yet were not part of their core business. Given these circumstances, clients who had either cash flow problems, exceptionally poor systems, were suffering strong competition or who needed to relocate, initially dominated the outsourcing of IT.

The outsourcing boom was therefore born on the back of the IT area and the unique circumstances experienced in IT during the latter part of the twentieth century.

In those early days of outsourcing, the clients and their IT service providers would both anticipate that a specialist in IT would be able to provide at least a comparable level of service to that which existed before the transfer. Equally they would expect that the service provider could do this profitably whilst producing a saving for the client. Nevertheless, it is doubtful if too many people at the time could imagine the potential savings from an outsourcing arrangement.

> the outsourcing boom was born on the back of the IT area

The typical service provider will try to ensure that by the end of the transition, i.e. when the relevant staff are finally transferred to the service provider's employment, all the initial changes deemed necessary to the system have been completed. The cost of providing the service from that point on is always going to be an unknown until it finally takes place. It is interesting to note, however, that most providers initially estimated that the likely savings would be something under 20 per cent, but gradually began to realize that even when apparently efficient IT departments were being transferred, the figure could reach 40 per cent or more. Obviously this figure will be shared in some way by both client and service provider.

When the outsourcing of finance departments first became a reality, new, would-be, service providers imagined that the total saving might be in the order of 15–20 per cent. Although actual results have varied enormously, total savings of 40 per cent have been achieved with this function also.

Many of the early outsourcing deals were disasters for one and sometimes both parties, and for a while it appeared that the lawyers were always going to be the greatest beneficiaries.

However, when the successful deals started to get publicity, it became apparent that there was a significant savings factor to be shared by both parties, if an efficient specialist service provider was involved and sufficiently motivated. Once this situation was understood, it became clear that outsourcing could not be ignored. How could it be, when articles appeared, endorsed by both parties to an outsourcing, which indicated it was possible for a client organization to obtain both an improved service and cost savings immediately after the transition and then look forward to further service improvements and savings in the future.

Consequently, outsourcing became a dominant feature of business in the 1990s with functions other than IT being outsourced. As the globalization of business increased and the World Wide Web began to evolve, the growth rate of all the externalization to outside specialist industries such as outsourcing and contract manufacturing took off at similar rates.

> the important factor that cannot be ignored is that all functions are now being outsourced and the rate at which new contracts are being created is increasing all the time

The important factor that cannot be ignored is that all functions are now being outsourced and the rate at which new contracts are being created is increasing all the time.

However, it is important to understand the various reasons why this growth is taking place. Certainly, there are still many clients signing outsourcing deals for the very reasons that started the modern boom in IT outsourcing. In other words, they have cash flow problems, need to relocate, or recognize that they have very poor, non-competitive systems.

A significant number of others have approached the situation from a very different angle. They have accepted the evidence put forward by a number of satisfied clients and their providers and reasoned that the service improvements, savings and, above all, continuous improvements claimed could only have been achieved by using external specialists. They have, therefore, approached the outsourcing concept with added value in mind and did so even where the relevant managers believed that they were already competitive with the functions concerned.

Getting good performance from a service provider

It will be obvious, though, that to get the sort of performance from a service provider that BP Exploration claimed, the following factors must be in place:

- the provider should be an established specialist in the function;

- the provider should be a 'Mecca' for top quality staff;

- careful consideration must be given to the location of the service facility and to the treatment of all staff;

- the client will need to be an important customer;

- the provider must be highly motivated to make continuous improvements.

If the provider is also a consultancy or even associated with a consultancy, or has other clients, the motivation will have to be strong enough to limit the degree to which key personnel are moved to other projects. Some movement of the provider's staff around the client base will be desirable but even a slight fall off in motivation, such as might happen if the provider strikes an even better deal with another client, could be very damaging.

Motivating the provider

In order to motivate a specialist service provider there will need to be some inducement that runs until the end of the contract. In addition there will need to be a firm indication that a further contract, at least as lucrative as the first one, is available for a job well done. At a minimum this will involve a risk/reward sharing arrangement whereby, beyond a certain level, the two parties share further savings or losses in some pre-agreed way. These partnership or value-added arrangements make up the bulk of the so-called win/win deals. Increasingly, the emphasis will be more concerned with continuous improvements to the service rather than just cost savings. A good example of this is the deal by which Rolls Royce Aero-Engines outsourced virtually all of its IT department to EDS. The key factor in this arrangement being the EDS pledge to keep Rolls Royce ahead of its competitors in the IT function.

It has often been relatively easy for the client organization to set out its terms. Typically, a minimum service is laid down, which will naturally be superior to what they are experiencing at the time. Then the maximum price is stipulated. Where a partnership arrangement is in prospect it would be normal for the client to look for a stable price over a four or five year contract that was no more and very likely less than their current costs. Once these two issues have been mulled over by the client organization's management, they will, initially at least, claim to be happy to share any further savings the service provider might achieve on a 50/50 basis.

It is certainly true that most current outsourcing success stories are based on risk/reward sharing deals between client and service provider. It would be equally true to say that the enormous growth of modern outsourcing is largely based on such arrangements. However, a number of the providers credited with producing top quality performances for their clients have apparently performed badly for other risk/reward sharing clients of roughly the same size and importance. I hope some of the reasons for this situation will become clear in the later stages of this book.

• • • • • • • • • • • •

Conclusion

Using the sword and gun analogy referred to earlier, it is reasonable to picture the conventional non-core internal function as the sword department. It has been around a long time and it is under growing pressure from those that argue that it is out of date because it confuses the importance of key processes. In addition, further attempts to improve performance do not appear to justify the collective effort made.

Against that the concept of externalizing to a specialist provider could be likened to the gun – it is a relatively new idea and is capable of continuous improvements. Why then should anyone persist with the sword when they could have the latest high tech gun?

One very good reason is that you might get the outsourcing version of a gun that is difficult to understand, where there is no manual and the help desk has continuous routing problems. In such circumstances it would be unpleasant to see your competitor approaching with a sword.

Nevertheless, the gun now exists, therefore you need to consider future options very carefully.

chapter 4

reasons for outsourcing the various business functions

• • • • • • • • • • • • • • •

IT outsourcing

Perhaps the single most important reason for outsourcing IT is the chronic and almost continuous shortage of suitably skilled staff. Organizations based in or near major centres of population like London often feel that they are at the greatest risk of losing key staff because the best people will always want to work in the glamorous areas such as financial investment or the media and major centres of population provide the opportunity to pick and choose from a vast range of employers. Whilst accepting that organizations without an exciting image will probably be disadvantaged in this way, the fact is that the shortage is global – even the glamour organizations have IT recruitment problems.

> perhaps the single most important reason for outsourcing IT is the chronic and almost continuous shortage of suitably skilled staff

Despite the mid 1990s speculation that the start of the new century would see, for the first time, widespread unemployment in the ranks of IT specialists, the shortage is likely to be continuous for some time to come. Without doubt, newly IT trained personnel are coming off the University and college production lines in ever increasing numbers in most countries, and this will clearly ease problems for many organizations if they are content to concentrate on existing technology. However, the problem in maintaining competitiveness is that if an organization is to keep abreast of its competition it must be using the most up-to-date technology and be prepared and able to cope with future developments. Simply having IT specialists is only part of the answer if they not being trained in relevant new developments.

A few people believe that the pressure to outsource IT will largely disappear over the next year or so. In Western Europe the amount spent on in-house IT and accounting functions is broadly similar – between 1.5 per cent and 4 per cent of turnover for the average company. As time goes by, most observers anticipate that IT expense will increase rather more quickly than that for finance. However, the fact that they are currently reasonably in line suggests to some optimistic individuals that IT costs may have stabilized and that further outsourcing of the function is not necessary.

On first investigation, the internal IT department looks like a sound concept. The organization can employ its own specialists in the quantity and quality it requires and these people will be available to carry out the specific tasks that are necessary each and every working day. Sadly, for most organizations this ideal concept is flawed due to the skills shortage and the accelerating changes brought on by new technology. Each organization needs to avail itself of the best service that information technology can offer. But the individuals with the skills necessary to bring about the very best service want to be involved with specialist organizations that can offer exciting work and the opportunity for personal development.

One ever present 'nightmare scenario' for many IT Directors is the need to take on new technology at a time when the ongoing workload is at stressful levels which effectively rule out or limit the chance of widespread re-training. If, as usually happens, some of the staff decide to move on during this period, then the nightmare becomes even more frightening.

The areas where the shortage of qualified IT specialists is now most acute include call centre design, ERP, internet development and data warehousing, all areas that have appeared on the scene relatively recently. The only thing we know about the future is that new specializations and applications are likely to appear at an accelerated rate. Therefore, there may always be a skills shortage relating to the newest developments.

The IT function is now clearly becoming increasingly important for all organizations and for a growing number of them more and more difficult to understand and use. The need to reduce costs, deliver faster cycle times and generally improve the service is going to become increasingly difficult to reconcile when considered against the needs of core activities.

Most sizeable organizations in the Western world now have a target saving of 30 per cent in mind when they begin to consider outsourcing IT. If they could achieve such a saving whilst obtaining a comparable or better service, then logically their management would find it difficult to argue against outsourcing, particularly if they believed that they were 'getting rid of a problem'.

One reason why there is not an automatic rush to outsource IT departments is that so many deals go wrong. It is variously estimated that 20–35 per cent of IT outsourcing arrangements are cancelled or not renewed when the contract is completed. I accept there are reasons why a contract may not be renewed other than client dissatisfaction with the service provider. Nevertheless, a significant number of IT outsourcing arrangements fall far short of keeping the client satisfied and competitive. This is the main reason for caution and improving overall understanding when contemplating such a venture.

> one reason why there is not an automatic rush to outsource IT departments is that so many deals go wrong

Another reason for caution is the fact that the outsourcing service providers, large and small, all find it difficult to find sufficient quality staff to meet their needs. Being IT specialists they will find it easier to recruit good people than their clients, because they offer increased promotion prospects, but they are probably growing much more quickly than other organizations which will act as a balancing factor. It may appear comforting that the service provider has hundreds or thousands of specialist staff on the payroll, but that does not mean that all or any of these people can be switched to your project at a moment's notice.

Consequently, the client organization should take careful note of how many of its own IT staff will stay with the provider after the transition. If the provider has to replace most of the team early in the arrangement, then there is cause for some concern. It is worth talking to the provider's last client and asking how frequently short-term contractors are moving in and out of the project. To be fair, though, some providers have done a good job in achieving a smooth transition and successfully implementing new systems on time even when they were unable to add as many specialists to the project as originally thought necessary. It would also be fair to add that if unforeseen problems do occur during the transition or at a later date during the contract, the typical IT service provider will logically have a better chance of overcoming them than the client would on its own.

An organization considering outsourcing a non-core IT function must look very carefully at what it might be giving away. Some organizations have retained the senior 10 to 15 per cent of staff in house and still found that they have handed over skills to the service provider which are key to its future wellbeing. If this happens then it will be very important to have set up a good relationship with the provider. Although losing valuable skills in this way does sometimes occur, this is not the same as sharing skills. It would be surprising if the provider's staff did not learn something new from working with the client organization, but that is not normally a problem because on the plus side each client will benefit from the ideas the provider has picked up from other clients.

Management differs strongly regarding potential loss of knowledge or skills. There are managers who fret about the use of contractors or consultants for fear that they could pick up information that will be given to other organizations and so damage the competitive situation. Other managers appear to believe that any knowledge or skills advantage they have is likely to be fleeting and therefore not worth trying to protect. However, the vast majority will recognize the need to be prudent with the organization's intellectual capital whilst accepting that there has to be some give and take.

The number of organizations which have suffered serious knowledge and skills losses from outsourcing IT must be relatively small. It would normally only occur where key individuals left the client but refused to join the provider, or the loss occurred somewhere in the system during the transition, i.e. as sometimes happens with lost legacy systems which are later found to be important.

In the past, organizations tended to outsource IT without considering loss of knowledge and skills as a serious problem – it was after all a non-core function and the desire or need to outsource was often an admission that there was not much at risk. If that was ever really true for the majority of organizations, there must be some doubt that it is still true today and serious doubt that it will be true tomorrow.

If the various business functions are pictured as branches on a tree, then when IT outsourcing got underway in the 1970s and 1980s, the IT branch was a relatively thin but quick growing limb. Even then, its enabling qualities had resulted in small shoots going out to other branches and giving the tree a lop-sided appearance. Since then the branch has become very strong, it is firmly attached to most of the other branches and entwines the trunk. In effect the IT branch could be likened to a parasite ivy plant apparently intent on strangling a giant oak. The ivy has a different agenda from the oak tree and the oak might be better off without it.

> is it possible that the typical IT department is strangling the organization and confusing its need to concentrate on core functions?

Is it possible that the typical IT department is strangling the organization and confusing its need to concentrate on core functions? Let's face it, functions like finance and HR would probably not be candidates for outsourcing if technology played no part in their operation.

All the various ways in which IT permeates an organization and the growing trend to integrate all the functions by the use of enterprise resource planning (ERP) systems does not mean that IT has become a core function but it might be even more difficult in time to outsource than a core function. In the past, management gurus have likened the chief executive or the board of directors to the business equivalent of the human brain. Few business brains could function without IT in today's competitive market and so any operation to remove and outsource these key links to the brain must be thought out very carefully. This does not mean that you cannot improve the brain's capability by outsourcing, but the subject is worthy of deep thought.

The usual reaction to the fear of outsourcing part of the organization's grey matter is to bring in the strategic argument. It sounds simple 'Keep the strategic technology in house and outsource the rest'. But what is strategic in IT terms? It's unlikely to be the most expensive hardware purchased because that's probably the mainframe 'rusting' in the shed. Is it the most recent hardware purchased, or the software systems currently in use or the combined skills and knowledge of the IT team? The strategic IT argument will be valid for many organizations but for others it is meaningless. Obviously it is possible to outsource parts of IT that are clearly defined entities such as legacy systems, desk top support, applications development, etc. However, as previously stated, IT has spread its tentacles right through the organization, therefore in many situations it would be difficult for anyone to separate the strategic elements.

In any case, why should all organizations want to outsource everything but the strategic element? Those organizations that outsource for the original negative reasons, i.e. poor systems, cash flow problems, etc. must anticipate getting an improved service from the outsourcing service provider. Why then separate what they consider to be the strategic systems and prevent them getting a better service?

I appreciate I have been making arguments both in favour and against outsourcing in the above paragraphs. But in all IT outsourcing situations there are arguments for and against. For most organizations the IT function continues to offer the greatest benefits from outsourcing, but also the greatest risk. With this function more than any other, the client needs to be confident that the service provider will strive to improve the service throughout the length of the contract. A risk/reward sharing partnership will go some way towards achieving this aim, but short of owning part of the provider's equity, how can the client guarantee it?

Business process outsourcing

Within the outsourcing industry, the term business process outsourcing (BPO) is used to describe the outsourcing of a varying mix of non-core processes. Typically this mix will include finance and accounting, HR, procurement, payroll, internal audit, taxation work, customer support centres and a range of industry specific processes. To some people BPO will also include applications processing. However, I prefer the definition given by Dataquest, an American IT research company. Dataquest looks at BPO as information technology enabled business processes, i.e. those processes that are IT intensive and/or should be IT intensive and can be transformed by the application of information technology. Since almost every business process is at least supported to some degree by information technology, this definition leaves a lot of grey areas. But basically the Dataquest definition would not include catering services; gardening services, etc. because they require little or no need for IT. On the other hand they see application outsourcing as IT outsourcing because typically it is the management of that application that is involved. Onsite or remote, Dataquest argues, it is an application management function and is therefore part of IT.

However the definition is drawn, it is clear that a significant proportion of major organizations in the developed world have now outsourced a large number of these processes. What is less clear is the degree of success achieved.

In 1998 PricewaterhouseCoopers commissioned Yankelovich Partners to carry out a global study on BPO. This study covered 304 top decision making executives in 14 countries. After confirming that global competition was the main driving force for indulging in BPO, 63 per cent agreed that they had outsourced one or more of the processes concerned. Of those that had outsourced, a very positive 84 per cent claimed to be satisfied with the performance of their service provider.

Few industry insiders will be unduly surprised by the above satisfaction claims. Payroll is the most widely outsourced administrative process, it was one of the first areas to be outsourced and 97 per cent satisfaction levels have been recorded for payroll outsourcing alone in the recent past.

With the possible exception of finance and accounting, all the other business processes are less dependent on state of the art technology being used in the outsourcing than the IT function itself would be. Perhaps it would be more correct to say that the absence of the latest technology is not so transparent in some of these processes. For example, a CEO or FD may be more than happy to see that payroll costs are on a gradually reducing scale, without realizing that even greater savings might have been possible if the service provider had utilized the latest technology improvements. The client not being aware of the technology improvements being made also means that over time the provider could be passing on a declining proportion of the savings being made.

Nevertheless, few would deny that there is reasonable level of satisfaction amongst most client organizations that have outsourced business processes. This also appears to be true even where savings of under 10 per cent are the norm and where credible service providers are more thin on the ground than in the IT market.

> despite this reasonable level of satisfaction, the growth in BPO always seems to lag behind the forecasts made

Despite this reasonable level of satisfaction, the growth in BPO always seems to lag behind the forecasts made. On a global basis, government departments have been responsible for a significant amount of BPO, but this has never been copied to the same extent by the private sector. Some of the main service providers are handling what are very similar and essentially simple processes for a wide range of public sector clients in many countries around the world. In many cases the providers are dealing with these processes in more or less the same way that their clients did. They might have improved the service since taking it over but they are still concentrating on making the service fit in with related services for the client concerned. At some point these service providers will need to independently design process specific ways of doing the work and then set about convincing their clients of the advantages. Admittedly, it will be more difficult to do this for some processes than it is with, say, payroll, but it may be essential before major expansion in the private sector can be achieved. In time I would expect a number of service providers to offer niche services on a package basis within the BPO marketplace.

Any client organization contemplating outsourcing one or more business processes would be well advised to build in safeguards from day one. This will include benchmarking the current service and doing it in such a way that the in and out of scope boundaries are clearly defined. The various appendices to this book outline the safeguards that should be taken when dealing with the service providers and include arguments for and against going with a sole provider or creating a competition. This latter point is particularly important in BPO because many arrangements start with the client talking to one provider about one function and end many months later in an agreement with that provider to take over a range of functions on an integrated basis. The client management may have been willing to work on a sole provider basis for the original amount of work but would have instinctively tried to create a competition if they had only realized just how much was eventually going to be outsourced to one provider. It is natural that as the talks develop the service provider will explain how the client's competitive position can be improved by including more processes in the mix. Obviously, the client organization is not going to outsource if it is not going to benefit. However, the question remains – would they have increased the benefits obtained in the outsourcing if they had created a competition?

It has sometimes been argued that as the various elements making up BPO are not so technology dependent as IT, then the need to outsource these areas will decline when the overall economy goes off the boil. It would be surprising if this were true. Outsourcing has increased all over the world during both periods of economic expansion and decline. Clearly, most outsourcing to date has involved IT and it is easier to imagine why IT would appear as a candidate for externalization in periods of both growth and decline. Nevertheless, BPO has taken place all through the relatively high growth period of the late 1990s. As the cost savings issue is likely to come to the fore in periods of economic decline, BPO will presumably continue to be practised.

None of this quite explains why BPO always seems to grow less quickly than most observers anticipate. Perhaps the real reason for this is that many senior managers instinctively realize that until the future of their IT is really on a sound footing then outsourcing a significant number of BPO operations is tantamount to putting the cart before the horse.

It is worth looking at some of the functions included in BPO in more detail.

Finance outsourcing

One statistic that appears quite frequently in the trade press is that about 50 per cent of sizeable UK organizations have outsourced a significant part of their IT. We are also led to believe that in the average organization, IT and finance account for similar levels of expenditure. Therefore, if outsourcing was always carried out on the purely strategic basis of externalizing non-core functions; it would be reasonable to expect finance to be outsourced as often as IT.

In recent times a significant number of multinationals, including BP, Shell, National Starch & Chemical, Sears, NFC, Conoco, Lasmo and a range of public sector organizations have outsourced finance and accounting. There are many more in the pipeline and a number of SMEs have recently found suitable providers – often with IT and finance going as a package in one contract. Nevertheless, it is extremely unlikely that finance and accounting will ever be outsourced as frequently as IT. Most informed guestimates see a maximum of 15 per cent of all organizations outsourcing finance by 2005.

There are many reasons for believing that finance outsourcing will always lag behind IT outsourcing. Some of these reasons are obvious and some less obvious. Many organizations find it almost impossible to recruit top quality IT staff because their systems are

> there are many reasons for believing that finance outsourcing will always lag behind IT outsourcing

old and 'uninteresting', they cannot afford competitive salaries and promotion prospects are limited or non existent. It is difficult to imagine a direct comparison with finance, although clearly 'high flying' accountants are more likely to be attracted to organizations experiencing high growth, etc.

The factors leading to the growth of finance outsourcing are summarized below.

1 For major multinational clients the prospect of transferring the finance function to a 'Big Five' consultancy can appear very attractive. When finance outsourcing was first treated seriously in the early and mid 1990s, the partners in several of these major accountancy-based consultancies made a big effort to inform all of their senior contacts in major client companies that they were ready, willing and able to meet the challenge of being a service provider should it arrive. In addition the impression was given that the service improvements and savings could be significant.

2 The Big Five appeared to offer the prospect of being service providers who could not afford to fail. The assumption was that these providers would not risk losing their hard earned reputations and so whatever the problems encountered they would 'throw money and people' at them until they were sorted out. Sadly, events in a couple of outsourcing relationships would appear to have shattered this belief.

3 The promise of improved service levels, savings, freeing up management time to allow concentration on the core activity and other perceived benefits puts pressure on finance directors to at least consider this option. Accenture (previously Andersen Consulting) and PricewaterhouseCoopers can both point to major clients that enjoy finance and accounting costs that are currently 50 per cent less than before the service was transferred.

4 For SMEs, in particular, there is often the prospect of outsourcing IT and finance in one package to a single provider.

5 In theory at least, finance outsourcing offers the Big Five and other large accountancy-based firms the chance to boost growth and profits. These prospects come at a time when audit fees are constantly being squeezed and other sections of the firms see similar difficulties ahead.

6 Finance outsourcing will allow the accountancy-based service providers a greater utilization of specialist skills across the firm.

7　Finance outsourcing may be unique in that the largest potential providers already have the staffing and infrastructure necessary to attack the market whilst, unlike IT outsourcing, they are not required to outlay large sums of money for equipment.

8　Finance outsourcing creates consultancy opportunities in the short, medium and long term – conversely if another provider gets in, these opportunities may well be removed during the life of the contract.

9　All other things being equal, the prospective client will lean towards the provider who has the experience. Therefore, in the short term there are bound to be special efforts made by the would-be providers who have not yet won enough contracts, possibly resulting in greater than normal discounting and equally major efforts by the providers who have won contracts to keep the others out.

The circumstances would appear to exist therefore, for a great deal of marketing and promotional effort to take place in support of outsourcing the financial function. The senior partners in at least two major providers have suggested that they would be prepared to give up the audit of a client company in order to become its financial outsourcing service provider. However, there is increasing pressure, particularly from the USA, that auditing firms should not be involved in providing other services to clients. It will be interesting to see how each of the Big Five reacts to this pressure in pursuing outsourcing deals.

Over the last few years of the 1990s, European finance directors have been amongst the most prolific attendees at outsourcing training courses and have instigated a large number of outsourcing enquiries. Experience now suggests that much of this apparent interest was done for defensive reasons, i.e. the finance directors wanted to learn as much as possible about the subject in order to stop it happening. I am aware of a number of cases where the finance director has been instrumental in involving service providers and advisers using the carrot of outsourcing the finance function, only to use his or her own special position in the organization to outsource some completely different function.

The unusual features that created IT outsourcing, i.e. having existing heavy investment in hardware and systems and needing to move to other expensive hardware and systems, can be seen as a problem peculiar to large organizations. Part of the same problem – needing to purchase and implement new financial or ERP systems – can be seen as a major reason for outsourcing finance but it is by no means the only one.

The UK government's desire to bring competition into the public sector has led to substantial financial outsourcing contracts being signed in local government, central government and the health sector. The creation of the Private Financing Initiative (PFI) by which large scale computer and related systems can be purchased under 30 year contracts for services instead of purchasing the assets has also increased outsourcing activity over the range of IT the UK government's desire to bring competition into the public sector has led to substantial financial outsourcing contracts being signed in local government, central government and the health sector

and BPO areas. Overall this government-inspired activity must be one of the key reasons for the interest in finance outsourcing in the UK and may well have sparked desire in one or two private sector organizations.

During the 1990s Andersen Consulting grew more quickly in Europe than the other members of what is now the Big Five. By the mid 1990s Andersen Consulting was the only one of these firms directly involved in outsourcing IT as service providers. By about 1995 the other big firms were very much aware that Andersen had gained significantly increased consultancy work in the IT area as a result of having tied clients. In other words, if they had not been involved as an IT service provider some of this work would have gone to other consultancies. They also saw that the major outsourcing service providers such as EDS had grown their consultancy teams very quickly at a time when their own growth was only moderate. Naturally, they again surmised that at least some of this growth must be attributed to the tied clients' factor. For some providers then, growth in consultancy and outsourcing is very closely linked and for this reason we must expect some major consultancies to be continually on the look out for new finance outsourcing business.

At the time of writing, the most recent major finance outsourcing deal in the UK involved Safeway, the country's fourth largest supermarket company, and PricewaterhouseCoopers. In this deal PWC has obtained a £60 million, ten year arrangement to run Safeway's internal finance and accounting department from 1 July 2000. More than 350 Safeway personnel dealing with accounts payable, accounts receivable, stock and margin accounting, payroll, financial accounting and insurance and property accounting were then transferred to PWC. This contract was won after keen competition from other major accountancy-based consulting firms and is unlikely to be the last major deal of this type.

Call centres

The call centre concept is relatively new and already it is getting a very bad press. There are certainly some very bad call centres that subject the users to time-wasting ordeals. Typically the users' problems start with a message telling them that due to the excellence of their product or service all their operatives are very busy just now, but not to worry because they are very special and are in a queue. Then while they wait they are entertained with offensive noises. Next they are subjected to numerous requests to press various digits for services they don't want and end with a disappointing discussion with someone who is difficult to understand and cannot begin to grasp the nature of the problem.

The call centre theory is based on the sound principle of the people answering the telephones being able to access all relevant information via the PCs in front of them. Why, then, do the services appear to deteriorate the higher one goes up the technology chain? Computer manufacturers and internet service providers will argue that the complicated nature of their business means that some customers will always raise problems that are difficult to solve and that routing and other traffic problems are bound to happen occasionally due to rapid growth. Fair enough, but why is there a general perception that high tech help desks are not improving and that some of the companies have lost interest in this aspect of their service? By comparison, call centres operated by insurance companies, investment houses and banks do appear to have improved quite markedly in recent times.

Setting up call centres and operating them well is nowhere near as straightforward as some people assume. For those organizations that understand and overcome the problems involved there is considerable scope to offer outsourcing services to others. Housing associations, for example, are constantly on the receiving end of telephone calls made by their tenants and potential tenants. The average housing association is too small to set up its own specialist call centre, yet the number and type of calls are suited to the call centre concept. At the time of writing, no one has come forward with an independent call centre alternative that would spread the costs over a range of such associations.

> setting up call centres and operating them well is nowhere near as straightforward as some people assume

The logic for outsourcing call centre work is compelling. Providing the service and cost are both acceptable, why go to the considerable trouble of building your own call centre from scratch when you could simply take space in an existing unit where the initial teething troubles have long since been overcome? In addition, it is much too early to assume that the typical call centre model is easily defined. Many call centres are being restructured into Contact Centres in which communication can additionally be achieved via emails and WAP phones.

The risks involved in call centre outsourcing appear to be very limited when compared to other functions and therefore it is likely that this area will see considerable growth over the next few years. However, call centre outsourcing clients must recognize that the people at the end of a telephone in a remote call centre may be playing a major part in the image the organization is projecting to its customers. For that reason they may feel the need to directly employ some or all of the supervisory staff. It will also be necessary to monitor the service being provided and to compare it on a regular basis with the service being provided by competitors.

Human resources outsourcing

Mention human resources outsourcing and you often end up talking about two different subjects. To some it means outsourcing the specific function, i.e. dealing with health and safety issues, working conditions, employee discipline, etc. within the client organization. Others use the term to describe the concept of outsourcing a group of workers, who are not already part of an outsourcing arrangement, to a specialist third party service provider.

I propose taking this latter concept first in order to get rid of it quickly. I understand that specialist IT companies have been known to transfer the employment of all non directors to human resources companies that have established recruitment skills in IT. Clearly, these client organizations take this action because they have difficulty finding and retaining qualified people. There is, therefore, some logic in transferring this responsibility to a specialist organization that in theory at least has access to many specialists. Even so, I see a potential problem here in that an organization adopting this policy may be relying on 'contractors' for long-term roles where a dedicated employee would be more suitable. Looking outside the IT function, it is difficult to see this concept becoming widely practised. If an organization wants to move further along the 'virtual' road, it would, in most instances, be preferable to transfer each group of employees along with their respective functions to specialist service providers in those functions.

Outsourcing the human resources department is not that different from outsourcing any other function in terms of the problems to be faced. However, there is one factor that makes it difficult for most organizations to contemplate such action. The HR department is involved with issues that are critical to the wellbeing of the entire workforce and to outsource those responsibilities will normally be seen as a strong indication to all concerned that the management does not rate these issues highly. In addition, it is important to think about the effect on the employees being transferred. They should play the caring role in the organization. Will they care as much if they are outsourced or, more importantly, will they be perceived as caring as much? In addition, once they are outsourced, will they lose contact with the corporate philosophy or culture? Will they adjust to their new employer's culture?

Major organizations appear to be constantly reducing the number of employees on their payrolls – a process that shows no sign of slowing down. Nevertheless, for most organizations their employees will remain one of their most important assets. When redundancies abound it becomes even more important to make sure that the organization is perceived as being interested in the welfare of the remaining staff. It is natural in the period following major redundancies for employees to want to check out various elements of their benefits and sadly this often coincides with a dramatically increased workload in the HR department. In such an environment of distrust and fear even the introduction of interactive technology that allows employees to update their benefits arrangements, retirement contributions and payroll deductions may sometimes be seen as a sign that senior management does not care.

None of the above factors can be taken as proof that outsourcing the HR function is always right or always wrong. They do, however, suggest that great care must be taken before steps that cannot easily be corrected are put in place.

For major organizations the 'natural' HR service providers will be the major international consultancies – several are actively pitching for such work. And yet over the last few decades these consultancies must have under-performed the rest of industry in HR management by a very long way. Excessive staff turnover in the HR departments of these major consultancies has been the norm for a long time and HR management has often been a sinecure for tired or failed partners. Having said that, I have to admit that if I were under pressure to outsource a major HR department I would be drawn to considering these firms. Let's face it, these organizations employ bright people and they ought to be able to create top class HR services using the latest technology.

Finally, it is worth remembering that in most of the developed world the client is rarely able to transfer full responsibility for staff simply by outsourcing them and placing them on another organization's payroll. Given these factors I would not expect an enormous rush amongst established organizations to outsource this function. I would, however, expect some growth in HR outsourcing companies that make most of their income from providing specialist personnel managers on a part-time basis to small companies.

. . . .

Facilities management

Third party management of property and other physical assets has a long history and was certainly well established before the outsourcing of IT became popular in the late 1970s and 1980s. As much of the original IT outsourcing was largely based on physical assets like mainframes, it was natural for many people to talk in terms of facilities management or FM when describing IT outsourcing. Gradually, however, the term FM became confined, as far as IT is concerned, to situations where legacy hardware and systems are maintained by third party organizations in a run down mode.

Facilities management as it relates to property continues to expand and in many Western countries third party specialists manage the vast majority of major buildings and business sites. Facilities management specialists now offer a wide range of services including planned maintenance, estate management, landscape management, new building project planning, benchmarking and relocation management.

It is difficult to imagine anything but further growth in facilities management because fashion or trends in other business areas have not, so far, affected its success. For

> it is difficult to imagine anything but further growth in facilities management because fashion or trends in other business areas have not, so far, affected its success

example, in the UK many areas of outsourcing have been given a boost by the government's policy of privatization. That is certainly not true of facilities management. In mid 1999 it was announced that Trillium, a partnership between Mitie and Goldman Sachs, won the contract to run the 700 buildings belonging to the Department of Social Security. This was the first transfer of UK government properties to the private sector, but other government departments are now showing various levels of interest in the concept.

Outsourcing from inside the industry

It is sometimes possible for an organization to become a service provider for its competitors and still be in competition with them in other areas. The financial services sector is currently throwing up a number of interesting examples of client organizations that are seeking competitive salvation by outsourcing services to apparent competitors and others that are happy to adopt the service provider role.

Churchill Insurance has adopted a service provider role in certain parts of the UK insurance business. As an example, United Assurance recently outsourced its general insurance business to Churchill Insurance. In this deal, United Assurance will continue to sell general insurance products but they are underwritten and serviced by Churchill. The servicing responsibilities taken on by Churchill include telesales, policy servicing and claims handling.

Within the retail banking industry there is a small but growing trend for some banks to provide a range of business processing services to other competing banks. This can happen when a bank is in 'start-up' mode in a new location, when entering a new area of business or simply because competitive pressure makes it the best option. This type of service provider is becoming a factor in other areas of the banking industry. For example, in the investment banking industry Deutsche Bank has been providing a range of BPO services for Abbey National Treasury Services since 1995. Deutsche Bank claims that in certain areas of investment banking it has enabled Abbey National to act as a virtual bank, because it has been able to set up a trading business without having to build the delivery mechanism.

It is interesting to speculate how this practice might develop. There are some people in the banking industry who believe that the European banks will have to pay a high price for the efforts they were forced to make over the late 1990s in order to become Euro and Y2K compliant. They argue that in the rest of the world this time was largely spent improving the flow of transaction processing by adopting newly available technology. The obvious conclusion from this is that the European banks have a lot of catching up to do if they are to achieve a reasonable competitive standing.

Any sizeable organization that realizes that it is in danger of falling behind in the competitive stakes must seriously question its chances of catching up. Whatever the industry it must be accepted that catching up now will be much more difficult to achieve than at any time in the past. Just when you have installed and implemented the latest technology to gain the competitive edge you find your competitors are moving on to the next development. More positive managers will reason that once their competitors have implemented the next year's technology developments, they will, in turn, enjoy a competitive advantage for only a short period of time. The sceptics will counter this by pointing out the damage that could result in the meantime. This is the classic scenario that causes organizations to think about the main alternatives to going it alone – sharing services with competitors, outsourcing or preparing the company for acquisition.

The banks, of course, are suffering the brunt of the technology revolution. The advent of telephone banking alone would have been sufficient to bring about dramatic reductions in the number of branches remaining open. But the television and internet potential raises all manner of questions about the future nature of banking that cannot be fully answered at this point in time.

Obviously, the mergers and acquisition alternative will continue to play a part in the future, just as it has done in the past. If a bank does not fall victim to an acquisition, its management will be hoping that some magical new marketing initiative will be developed that will dramatically increase business – it's always far easier to obtain improvements and savings when business is booming. If the marketing breakthrough is not forthcoming then we are back to improving competitiveness by either internal project, sharing services with other banks or outsourcing.

The banking industry has probably gone through more internal performance improvement projects than any other sector. As a result, I would expect that senior executives in the large banks would now look at the prospect of carrying out major new internal projects with some trepidation.

> the banking industry has probably gone through more internal performance improvement projects than any other sector

The creation of industry-shared service centres, where each participating bank contributes according to its size and needs but no one bank acts as the service provider, will probably win some advocates. To make a success of an arrangement like this it will be necessary to create a separate joint venture under independent management.

The outsourcing option is probably more difficult for the banking sector than it is for other sectors because it is always going to be more difficult to split the processes into convenient packages that can be distributed between different providers. Given this situation it is difficult to see anything other than an existing bank being able to offer complete BPO services to the industry. This leads to the fascinating idea that some existing banks might eventually reposition themselves as service providers.

● ●

Contract manufacturing

Contract manufacturing is yet another facet of outsourcing that is bursting out in all directions. Just think of all the products on the supermarket shelves around the world featuring the supermarket's own label. In the early days of contract manufacturing the supermarket's own branded products were probably manufactured by companies manufacturing and selling well-known competitive brands on nearby shelves. Now companies who do not have branded products of their own do much of this manufacturing.

Electronics is another area that has been transformed by the activities of the contract manufacturers. Many of Europe's original computer manufacturers collapsed or moved into other areas of the computer business in the 1980s and early 1990s because they could not manufacture to the desired quality and price. Within a few years they were replaced by scores of new manufacturers such as Time Computers Ltd and Tiny Computers Ltd in the UK. The contract market for electronics had moved on to the stage where these new companies are effectively assemblers of parts made by other organizations around the world. This situation enables the Tiny Computers of this world to concentrate on their core activity of dealing with customers, safe in the knowledge that almost all new technology developments will be available to them on demand.

Therefore any entrepreneur with a good idea and access to capital can buy the manufacturing capacity and the non-core services such as distribution and finance that are necessary to run what appears to be a manufacturing business. In the electronics examples above it has been argued that Tiny Computers outsourced its core function and became a virtual company. In reality the company's core business is dealing with customers through retail shops and direct mail, so they have not outsourced their core function and they are not a virtual company.

Contract manufacturing of electronic components is a very big business. Various US estimates suggest that on a global basis it is worth $70 billion annually and is growing at between 15 and 20 per cent a year.

Some contract manufacturers are relatively new companies, created because entrepreneurs saw an opportunity. Some began as small assembly shops operating as sub-contractors to larger companies, others were set up by existing giants in the marketplace. Boots Contract Manufacturing, or BCM, for example, was the brainchild of Boots the Chemist, the UK high street chain of chemists. BCM is now the largest contract manufacturer of pharmaceutical products in Europe.

In the same general market, other providers have become more specialized than general contract manufacturers. Oxford Asymmetry International, for example, provides outsourcing services for pharmaceutical and biotechnology companies but concentrates on early drug development and production for clinical trials.

Insourcing

There are a variety of activities that might justifiably be called insourcing. SAGA, the established UK supplier of holidays to the over-50s, realized a number of years back that its database was an extremely valuable asset. In recent years it has benefited from the fact that it contains names and addresses of relatively wealthy people of mature age who are statistically less likely to have car accidents or incur damage to their property than their younger and perhaps less well-off counterparts.

> there are a variety of activities that might justifiably be called insourcing

SAGA argued that as a group these mature clients ought to benefit from cheaper insurance in these areas. This knowledge has enabled them to take a significant share of both the UK household insurance and car insurance markets. Recently the company extended its new range of services to include credit cards, gas supply, electricity supply, electrical goods, share dealing, investment schemes, savings schemes and dietary supplements.

SAGA is effectively the front for the front office organization, with much of the actual work being done, originally at least, by long established insurance companies, who deal directly with the client from the first telephone call onwards. The temptation will be for organizations that add new services in this way to do more and more of the work in house to maximize its own profit. Whether this would be a wise move remains to be seen and depends to a large extent on the tactics used.

In the same way, supermarket groups such as Sainsbury and Tesco have capitalized on the fact that shoppers increasingly visit out of town stores on a one-shop basis. The large stores and the resulting great range of products and services on sale, together with the out of town factor have all made it difficult to visit more than one shop on a single shopping trip. These supermarket groups are taking advantage of this situation in a number of ways. Perhaps the most startling is the venture into retail banking. The supermarket groups have a number of advantages over the traditional banks in that the customer is already on the premises and can often obtain additional cash without the trouble and cost of writing out a separate cheque. A favoured customer can write one cheque or provide a one card transaction that covers both purchases and any additional cash required. Major and long established banks do the actual banking behind the scenes, but most if not all the customer contact comes via the supermarket employees.

The major banks are being forced to close branches on a regular basis because of new banking alternatives. These banks also have extensive records of individuals and they have added information about real income levels. It is therefore possible that some of these banks may fight back by selling other goods and services via the internet.

Insourcing has been used as a way of safeguarding a marketplace. Imagine a situation where a specialist manufacturer of plastic paint coverings has a long established exclusive contract to supply its product to a major international company that has found increasing benefit from coating more and more of its products in plastic. The contract has gradually become a major part of the plastic company's business and with this has come awareness that loss of the contract would put its future existence in doubt.

Given this situation, it would be reasonable to try to establish a further long-term arrangement with the customer well in advance of the original contract ending. Knowing that any follow up contract is likely to be decided largely on price, a number of organizations in similar circumstances have adopted the insourcing formula to safeguard themselves. They therefore, offer the customer a number of 'outsourcing' benefits even though the work continues in the customer's premises as before. These benefits will probably include a price that will be stable over time, plus a quality and delivery guarantee of some description. In order to provide these guarantees the supplier will probably request that certain employees be transferred to its payroll, even though there is little likelihood of the individuals concerned working away from their current site.

In theory, at least, this type of arrangement can benefit the customer in terms of cost, delivery, quality and peace of mind, whilst safeguarding the supplier's future.

Software maintenance support

one area of outsourcing that more and more companies are considering is software maintenance

One area of outsourcing that more and more companies are considering is software maintenance. Typically software companies charge an annual fee of 15–20 per cent of their 'list' prices for maintenance.

Maintenance coverage usually includes:

- hot line telephone support

- fixes to reported software bugs

- upgrades to the latest software releases.

Maintenance represents a substantial portion of all software suppliers' revenues. In fact, many suppliers have been able to survive slow periods solely on their maintenance fees.

However, if you analyze how software suppliers spend their maintenance revenue, you discover that the majority of maintenance is spent on developing new software releases and only a relatively small portion is spent on providing hotline or bug fix support.

Like all products, software goes through a lifecycle. Therefore, when a user organization decides that it does not want to purchase any more upgrades of a software product, they should consider outsourcing their maintenance to a third party. Software supplier maintenance, at this stage of the lifecycle, is often a waste of money because the user organization:

- is on a very stable version of the product;

- rarely reports any new problems to the supplier;

- is usually told by the supplier to upgrade to later releases to fix any outstanding problems;

- has no intention of spending time and resources upgrading.

Expert third-party maintenance support organizations have evolved which provide software 'insurance policies' that guarantee organizations receive expert advice and support in times of need. One such company, Centaur Application Software Services, claims that the cost of third-party maintenance can be as little as 15 per cent of the cost of the supplier's maintenance fees. Another advantage of third-party maintenance is that organizations can tailor the support to their own unique needs instead of accepting the supplier's usual maintenance terms and conditions.

Outsourcing software maintenance means that organizations only pay for the support and insurance that they actually need. They are no longer paying for the development of new software releases they never intend to use.

Outsourcing marketing functions

In some organizations, business functions and processes may be deemed prime candidates for outsourcing simply because they are not core to the organization's main activities. Some functions or processes like payroll, for example, are not only non-core but also the transaction activity is irregular and can be confined to certain periods of the month. In these circumstances most people can see the advantages of outsourcing. Yet other functions are not only non-core and used infrequently, but they require specialist skills that cannot normally be justified for a single enterprise

Into this category come a variety of legal services and a range of marketing activities such as advertising and market research. Most advertising and market research work is done on an external basis with only a relatively small number of major organizations attempting to duplicate these services in house. Advertising agencies in particular need to develop specialist skills in a range of areas, from design of advertisements to media buying and dealing with artists and performers used in commercials. To all intents and purposes, advertising is as fully outsourced as its ever likely to get and the same might be said for some of the services relating to advertising. For example, one company, Donovan Data Systems, supplies 98 per cent of all the computer systems and back up used by European advertising agencies, and has almost the same penetration in North America.

Throughout most of the twentieth century generalized sales organizations have existed that were prepared to provide additional teams of sales people to any organization that might require them. Typically a company needing to increase its sales activity would employ one or more of these sales people in special sales drives aimed at householders or retailers. By the 1950s and 1960s specialist teams were developing in the Western world that concentrated on a particular marketplace and therefore were perceived as up-market operations. The prime example in the UK was Food Brokers Ltd, which as the name suggests, concentrated on selling to the supermarkets and other retailers that included food and related products amongst their wares. The outsourcing of sales activities utilizing people on a face to face basis, did not increase very much over the last half of the twentieth century and there is little evidence that further growth is in the offing.

> marketing departments are being outsourced, but not in sufficient numbers to indicate that a significant trend is taking place

Marketing departments are being outsourced, but not in sufficient numbers to indicate that a significant trend is taking place. This area is sufficiently sensitive and important for most organizations to suggest that outsourcing ought perhaps to be confined to situations where the client can obtain an equity stake in the service provider.

chapter 5

• •

variations on the outsourcing theme

Value added partnership

At a time of unprecedented change there are obvious problems in setting rigid contracts. How can any organization be certain enough of its IT requirements over a four or five year contract? How can anyone be certain that the desktop equipment currently in use will not be out of date in just two or three years' time?

Nevertheless, I accept that there are a small number of client organizations who will feel that the function or group of processes to be outsourced is pretty stable – nothing much has changed over the last ten years, why should it change over the next ten? Where there is such confidence that change will not be a problem, then and only then, should a client organization contemplate a rigid contract. For the vast majority of situations, however, the outsourcing will take place in an atmosphere of future uncertainty.

Of necessity then, outsourcing arrangements ought to be flexible enough to allow for accelerated change, whether that change comes from technology, market changes or the client organization's market share.

> outsourcing arrangements ought to be flexible enough to allow for accelerated change, whether that change comes from technology, market changes or the client organisation's market share

The value added partnerships all have one thing in common – the 'risk/reward' element. Some of the very early outsourcing deals were so rigid that they allowed for almost no change to take place during the life of the contract. This enabled service providers, who may have been working on very tight margins to increase their profits significantly when charging for extras. Clients, who because of acquisition or growth in core business asked the provider for 20 per cent more work and expected a 20 per cent increase in charges, were often outraged when providers wanted to increase the charge by 50 per cent or more. Typically, independent assessors used to estimate the fair additional cost to be somewhere between the warring parties' own estimates. Obviously, change is not just something that happens as a result of growth or acquisitions. Consequently, extra and special tasks are part of the outsourcing service provider's lot and payment for these tasks can be a very delicate issue.

In theory, risk/reward partnerships enable the client to offset the risks implicit in a rigid contract by offering the provider a deal that restricts increases or decreases in charges to some pre-agreed formula in exchange for a share in measurable improvements that the provider makes to the service. In reality, human nature being what it is, the service provider often strives to remove most of the risk and the client does the same with the reward. For that reason not all risk/reward contracts achieve what was originally intended.

Nevertheless, for an outsourcing to be successful in both the short and long term, the service provider must be offered a carrot as well as a big stick.

The service provider's shared service centres

Quite naturally, most service providers see great benefits in setting up their own shared service centres (SSCs) where, for example, the business processes or IT functions of a number of clients can be handled under one roof. Clearly in this way the provider can maximize the economies of scale.

At first sight this concept has a lot going for it. A service provider setting up an SSC, for, say, finance would be able to keep adding to the list of organizations it was servicing from one location. In theory, therefore, this growth alone would go a long way to ensuring that the systems were being updated on a regular basis and that the latest technology was being used. It would also mean that design and implementation errors from the last project could be corrected more quickly than in the normal single function site.

Major providers like Accenture have in the past announced that they were setting up large SSCs in some central location from where they hoped to 'house' the services for new and unspecified clients.

Some providers have achieved a significant measure of success in promoting SSCs of this type, but for the most part clients are initially wary of such arrangements. The smaller client will start off by assuming that the larger clients will get an unfair share of the service. Against that the larger client imagines that if his or her service accounts for 50 per cent of the total, but there are five other clients – then they will get less service than they deserve and need.

Competing providers sometimes put an outsourcing service provider who wants to take the service away to another part of the country or to a different country, at a considerable disadvantage. This happens most often when providers who do not have their own SSC decide to stress the importance of the new outsourced facility being within walking distance of existing facilities.

> the provider-owned SSC is likely to play a growing part in outsourcing in the years ahead

The provider-owned SSC is likely to play a growing part in outsourcing in the years ahead. Major clients will often want to stipulate the exact location where the service will be delivered, but in most instances the provider will still be free to extend the business done in the SSCs by taking the work of smaller clients into the premises. For many of the BPO deals in existence the outsourcing only makes sense (at least from the service provider's point of view) if multiple arrangements can be brought together under one roof.

. . . .

The client's own shared service centre

The term SSC is most commonly used to describe attempts by major client organizations to centralize a function like finance by continent or even globally. Multinationals have always been concerned about the theoretical waste involved in having separate accounting and other services in all or most of their overseas subsidiaries.

Few of these major organizations had risked making any moves in this direction until the onset of the 1990s. But then communications and other technological advances reached a stage that made their desires a possibility. Elizabeth Arden, Union Carbide, Whirlpool and Mars had all centralized their accounts in one European country by the first half of the decade and many others have since followed suit. The European finance directors of many of the American multinationals now meet on a regular basis to swap ideas on how to improve the service from their SSCs. In effect, they have created a benchmarking club.

Tax advantages and the relatively low cost of employment may both be positive factors for centralizing in some countries whereas culture difficulties may be negative factors.

By the middle of the 1990s it was generally assumed that if a multinational carried out sound re-engineering of its total finance operation then it could achieve savings of around 30 per cent on what existed prior to the centralization. However, a widely held view also developed that a further 10 per cent may be possible for the client company if a major outsourcing service provider was involved to ensure continuous improvements.

Inevitably, this led to a number of arrangements where ostensibly the client organization started by trying to develop a global or continent-wide SSC to be run and managed entirely in house, but then changed tactics before the project ended. It was often a surprise to many people when the consultants helping with these changes were brought in as joint venture partners. Each new deal of this type appeared to differ quite significantly from the one before it.

For example when, in mid 1997, Shell Oil set about creating continent-wide SSCs for its finance area it eventually chose to enter into a 50/50 European partnership with the firm that had done its audit for over 100 years, Ernst & Young. The resulting joint venture is called Tasco Europe and is based in Glasgow.

Shell decided upon the SSC route after carrying out an extensive feasibility study. However, after taking into account the speed at which it needed to work and the consolidation work necessary over many individual companies across Europe, it decided to look for a partner. Six service providers expressed interest and Ernst & Young was chosen. Like most of the big accountancy firms at the time, Ernst & Young had only limited experience of actually doing day-to-day accounting transactions but it was very keen to get into the accounting outsourcing market.

Shell and Ernst & Young both fund 50 per cent of the joint venture and have equal representation on the board. However, every effort has been made to make Tasco independent. To begin with it had to 'sell' the benefits of the new service to each of Shell's 12 Western European subsidiaries.

Tasco has set itself a target of becoming the European market leader in accounting services. To do this it has to find new independent clients. Presumably, most of these clients are targeted to come from the ranks of the multinationals that have operations in different parts of Europe.

At the time of writing it would appear that Tasco Europe has made some significant progress both in integrating the services of the Shell subsidiaries and in its preliminary discussions with potential new clients. Nevertheless, I think that it will be some time before they can be sure that all the potential ongoing benefits have been achieved. In a conventional outsourcing arrangement the service provider will be expected to assume responsibility for the future design of systems. The provider will be seen as the specialist organization and the client's staff, both those retained and those being transferred, will usually accept the logic of the service provider's leadership. The risk inherent in these 50/50 SSC partnerships is that the leadership and responsibility for development direction is not always so clear-cut, even where the contract specifies each party's responsibilities. This will be particularly true where two strong teams are brought together as is the case with Shell and Ernst & Young. Therefore despite Tasco Europe starting off with a fistful of advantages, there will be some difficulties to overcome and it remains to be seen how successful this venture will be.

> the risk inherent in these 50/50 SSC partnerships is that the leadership and responsibility for development direction is not always so clear-cut, even where the contract specifies each party's responsibilities

• • • • • • • • • • • • • •

Joint ventures

The partnership between Shell and Ernst & Young was illustrated above to describe a shared service centre project. But it is also a good example of a client and a service provider coming together, initially to achieve a long-term competitive position for the client and then to make additional profit by selling the service to third parties. Other similar joint ventures include Connect 2020, set up by Andersen Consulting and Thames Water in 1995 to provide total supply chain management solutions to the utilities industries and other markets. The first customer was Thames Water but third party customers were targeted from an early date and by the end of the first year of operation Connect 2020 had won a number of new consultancy contracts. At about the same time Perot Systems, an IT and outsourcing services provider, set up a joint venture with East Midlands Electricity (now part of Powergen) and quickly obtained significant sales of the products they developed throughout Europe.

Joint ventures are also on the increase between outsourcing service providers. For example, Computer Sciences Corporation (CSC) recently joined with The IT Group, Inc, to form Mississippi Space Services (MSS) to provide facility operation services at NASA's John C. Stennis Space Center in Mississippi. Clearly, joint ventures created on this basis will normally be confined to working for just the original client. However, it is always likely that new products or services could be created during the ongoing development work that will have a ready market in the wider world. If this should happen and the client is agreeable, then presumably a separate joint venture would be formed with the client.

Some outsourcing service providers have created joint ventures without apparently first having a client in mind. For example, in late 1999, LOR Management Services, a Los Angeles-based provider of accounting and applications outsourcing services, announced a joint venture with AIL Technologies Inc, a designer and supplier of electronics, computer hardware, software systems and services. The agreement is intended to join LOR Management's expertise hosting clients' process-oriented accounting functions with AIL Technologies' computer hardware systems implementation and software development expertise. Quite obviously this arrangement has been created to enable the two companies to approach the market with a total IT and BPO service without having to merge their entire operations.

The development of the internet has already been responsible for a dramatic increase in the number of joint ventures being set up and this can only increase. In March 2000 Accenture, as it is now, and Microsoft Corporation announced a new joint venture called Avanade that, subject to regulatory approval, will deliver internet-specific and other enterprise platform services based on the Windows 2000 operating system platform. Under the $1 billion agreement, Microsoft will provide $385 million in cash to support Avanade, as well as solutions, development support and other intellectual capital. Accenture will provide intellectual capital, training, resources, solutions development and other services. Clearly, joint ventures are now being created in a variety of different ways depending upon the demands of the situation.

The subject covered in the next section – ASP outsourcing – is likely to spawn many such ventures.

• •

Application service provider outsourcing

Technology-driven change did not start with the internet but its evolution has resulted in an exhilarating, if frightening, lifestyle for senior IT managers. Managing an IT department of any size has always been a difficult job but the arrival of the internet appears to be making it a lottery. How can you plan for even the near future when new internet ventures appear to challenge the existence of everything you are working with and offer the prospect of doing everything quicker, better and more cost effectively, and yet, so far, relatively few of these magical solutions are proven and available?

One such solution, application service provider (ASP), might make the ERP concept of organization-wide integrated systems ultimately work for the many rather than the few. The big problem with enterprise resource planning systems is that because organizations need to customize between 15 and 30 per cent of the system, the implementation can take years rather than months. Normally implementation also involves costly outside help and causes considerable internal disruption. In any ERP implementation there is clearly a relationship between the time taken, the resultant attempts at short cuts (usually described by other names) and the risk of failure.

> the ASP concept has an outsourcing service provider delivering internet-based applications for a range of clients

The ASP concept has an outsourcing service provider delivering internet-based applications for a range of clients. Most current scenarios anticipate the ASPs developing from small and medium sized firms of consultants who specialize in a single or a small number of software packages. Against that, EDS also describes itself with every justification as an ASP. EDS maintains around 300 ERP related arrangements on a worldwide basis and appears very excited about the opportunities that Web hosting of major software products provides.

In the arrangements that have been put together so far, the ASP finds and builds the relationship with the client and supplies any 'local' hardware required. The link through the internet is then secured by entering into a partnership with the relevant software house and an internet service provider.

In this way the ASP takes responsibility for the implementation of the software, future system updating and support. In theory, this offers the client an 'externalization to outsourcing specialists' deal of enormous flexibility:

This added flexibility is due to a number of factors.

> **1** The ASP would be able to work for more clients per number employed than in a conventional outsourcing arrangement.
>
> **2** There is less need and justification for the very detailed work normally considered essential in setting up an outsourcing arrangement, i.e. all the work involved in the transition from producing service level agreements to the contract itself would be simplified because a system leasing deal is in place.

3　Compared with a conventional outsourcing, the ASP would benefit by doing much of the work on a repetitive basis for past, present and future clients and it would not be anywhere near as disastrous to lose a client.

4　The transitional consultancy time ought to be reduced.

5　Although much of the implementation of the new system and the ongoing running of it will have been outsourced, it will not feel like an outsourcing to the internal staff.

6　The opportunity will be there for the ASP to be made responsible for continuous improvements to the system. In fact, continuous improvements ought to occur almost automatically as the ASP works with new clients, then finds better and improved ways of working and updates existing clients with all improvements.

Taking these benefits into account, a number of ASPs have offered deals which have allowed their clients considerable flexibility in terms of contract length and have removed some or all up front costs in favour of a regular fee. The client connects to a server maintained by the ASP and uses the required software from that server on a monthly or annual fee basis. In theory the only software that will be required on the client's PCs will be a web browser. The ASP's server will run the application and so create the so-called 'thin' client solution.

Many of the world's leading computer companies such as Microsoft and IBM and communications giants like AT&T have taken, or are taking, steps to get involved with this marketplace. Most of the leading software vendors are either firmly entrenched or are playing with the concept. Some observers have expressed surprise at this interest because ASP deals will require renting or leasing arrangements instead of the highly profitable up front licences that have been one of the lynchpins of the packaged software industry to date. In reality, though, the major software vendors have no alternative but to cover each new development as it arises – if they don't, someone else will. The probability is that most major ERP software vendors are all frantically working to make their software packages Web-enabled server centric so that they can deliver thin client solutions. The thin client model is now the preferred software recommended by industry gurus to reduce the ever increasing total cost of ownership of fat client systems.

Against that, some industry observers firmly believe that at least two of these large software suppliers are desperately hoping that the ASP concept fizzles out somewhere along the way and well before they have been forced to invest heavily in it. To a large extent it will depend on how the software vendor perceives its own immediate future. Web enabling of software offers the large vendors a number of potential benefits including a possible reduction in the pirating problem, smoother, less costly marketing of updates and gives the customer, in theory, a chance to try the product before buying.

Some people argue that there are still significant problems to be faced, because the time taken to download the applications necessary with a major ERP currently makes the practice questionable in certain situations. Against that, there are many high speed downloading alternatives to the 56K modem and it would be surprising if downloading time turned out to be a limiting factor in the long run.

For the reasons given, the small and medium sized marketplace (SMEs) has been the main target for ASP activity and consequently the most enthusiastic software vendors are those supplying products for SMEs. However, even these software vendors don't appear to be totally convinced that they are taking a step that will be beneficial to them over the long term. It is fair to say that some of these software vendors fear that the development of the ASP concept will allow Microsoft to take a major share of this market. Equally, some of the fledgling ASPs fear that they could lose out in the long run to both the software vendors and the internet service providers. Considering this caution, it may be that the ASP concept would have not got going if it had not been for the dramatic 1999 downturn in business software sales.

Some of the internet service providers (ISPs) that direct their services to business users appear to be making a big effort to develop the ASP market. As it will be a relatively easy task for them to host major software applications, it appears too big an opportunity to ignore. Considering the facts available, it is difficult to see why the ISPs should not be successful in their attempts to build a major new market providing they get the desired interest from the marketplace. If they do not get such support they could be tempted to build their own software and create their own ASP teams. However, there is an enormous difference between managing a group of servers and providing business applications to the larger end of the business world. A new ASP will have to provide adequate support services from day one.

> some of the internet service providers (ISPs) that direct their services to business users appear to be making a big effort to develop the ASP market

Despite the promises of a rich new market for ISPs, software vendors and hardware suppliers, and cheaper and far shorter implementations, we cannot yet be certain that the ASP concept will achieve its undoubted potential. It will, after all, require a major effort by leading companies to bring about the necessary changes and many of the current leading players in this market, such as the large consultancies, are not really sure they will benefit from these changes.

If it does succeed, it will almost automatically provide clients with an advantage not found in any internal performance improvement projects and most outsourcing arrangements – the opportunity to remain competitive in the function or functions concerned. This will depend on the nature of the deal reached between the parties and the ASP's ability to regularly make improvements to the system. Nevertheless the opportunity would be there.

chapter 6

points to be aware of when choosing a service provider

The tendency to take on unsuitable work

In 1995 I was asked to talk to the management of a publishing group that claimed to be interested in outsourcing all its non-core functions. Most of the senior executives were at the meeting, with the exception of the chairman. During the first few minutes it became obvious that the chairman was the main instigator of the potential outsourcing project. It was also clear that roughly half of the directors present wanted a serious investigation to take place but the others appeared to be going through the motions.

Prior to my arrival they had agreed amongst themselves that it would be very beneficial in terms of limiting disruption, if one provider could take on all these non-core functions. I pointed out that the key reason for outsourcing was to take advantage of specialists in each function. One of the directors then introduced the name of a well known service provider and consultancy and although admitting no prior contact with the organization, expressed the view that 'they must have specialists in every conceivable business practice'. Despite my doubts, I was asked to contact the major provider and seek clarification that they would be willing to take on all the functions. I was asked not to divulge my client's identity at this time.

Amongst the functions being considered for outsourcing were finance, IT, human resources, the design studio and telemarketing. I was therefore, quite surprised when my contact at the major service provider came back to me stating that 'subject to the work not containing too many surprises, they saw no problem with taking on all the functions listed'. The only qualification was that they reserved the right to sub-contract certain functions to other suppliers if all parties deemed that beneficial.

The publishing group quickly gave up the idea of outsourcing and I am pretty sure that they have not given it serious consideration since that time. I cannot be sure that the offer to take on all the functions was the deciding factor but I am sure it played a part in the final decision. One or more of the directors concerned probably considered it a triumph of defensive tactics, whilst others would consider that the service provider got the just reward for greed.

Many providers would argue that greed does not come into the equation at all. Their justification for this view is that after a while the provider's core competence becomes the supply of an external service, whichever business processes that might involve. Certainly, there is evidence that providers have sometimes picked up work that was new to them, then got other

> nevertheless, for an outsourcing service provider, irrespective of size, there must be a significant risk that venturing into too many business areas will reduce the chance of it maximizing its performance in any one area

similar work on the back of it and eventually became competent specialists in that work area. Anyone who has been party to the range of processes and functions passed by government departments to individual private sector companies will confirm that this has happened quite frequently.

Nevertheless, for an outsourcing service provider, irrespective of size, there must be a significant risk that venturing into too many business areas will reduce the chance of it maximizing its performance in any one area. Any client organization seeking a service provider for outsourcing would be wise to look at where their potential providers are positioned in this respect.

It is important to make a distinction here between service providers taking on related functions, which is inevitable and unlikely to weaken creativity and effort, and unrelated functions, which could result in such weakness.

An example of related functions can be found in the insurance industry, where organizations like the Eastgate Group and Hampden Plc provide a mixture of IT, finance and a variety of insurance process services for companies in both run-off and start-up mode. Both these organizations became service providers as a result of the collapse of a number of Lloyds syndicates in the wake of the asbestos claims crisis. Effectively these syndicates were put out of business but they had to keep functioning to pay off debts. In a situation where there was no future remaining in the syndicates for ambitious executives, both companies were formed to take advantage of the situation and started covering all the related functions from day one. As a result both organizations have the experience and background to offer both finance and IT services to medium sized clients both inside and outside the insurance industry.

· ·

Use of sub-contractors

In the early stages of their outsourcing experience, clients tend to assume that the chosen service provider will do all the work to be transferred. However, in practice, sub-contracting plays an important part in a significant number of contracts and has done so since the early days of IT outsourcing. Consequently the sub-contractor issue is very likely to play a part in most arrangements at some stage.

Often the service providers will introduce the subject in a way that suggests that the functions or services to be dealt with on a sub-contracting basis are all non-critical. It may be argued that this is a perfectly reasonable opening 'sales' gambit even if they have every intention of eventually sub-contracting elements of work that most people would deem critical to the success of the overall service. After all, it is reasonable to assume that they would not consider the sub-contracting route if this were not in the best interest of maximizing the service. In addition, they might also argue that introducing this subject too early in the discussions is only going to cause unnecessary concern to the client when all past evidence would indicate that there is rarely any cause for concern if sub-contractors are handled correctly. Certainly the general industry view is that the use of sub-contractors has not in itself been the fundamental cause of failure on that many occasions.

Nevertheless, just suppose that the sub-contractor has been brought into the arrangement because the prime service provider does not have the basic skills necessary to perform certain key tasks. Given such circumstances, the identity and suitability of the sub-contractor is of vital importance to the client organization. The client organization must therefore be very aware from the early stages of the negotiations, as to exactly what role each and every sub-contractor will play. If there is any chance that poor or non-performance by an outsourcing sub-contractor will materially affect the service then the client must investigate the sub-contractor to the same depth that it is hopefully investigating the prime service provider.

The client must ensure that the service provider takes full responsibility for the work of the sub-contractor. The client should also ensure that it has the right to prevent any sub-contractor from providing goods or services to the organization if there is a perfectly reasonable cause for doing so. The client should also attempt to secure the right of replacing poorly performing sub-contractors.

. . . .

Size matters!

Ask any large client organization if it would be willing to outsource a key function to anything other than a major service provider and the answer will invariably be in the negative. There are a number of sound and obvious reasons for adopting this view but even taken together they do not prove that client and service provider should be of a similar size, or that a small service provider could not do a first class job for a much bigger organization, if the circumstances were favourable.

Most of the original IT outsourcing service providers such as EDS were already in existence as sizeable internal IT departments of major corporations. These internal departments were then re-invented as companies in their own right to take on a wider role to meet the outsourcing opportunity. Other early IT outsourcing service providers were often quite small organizations who just happened to have the right mix of skills at an opportune time. However, even these small providers were normally in a position to demonstrate that they had greater in-depth skills than the IT department that was being transferred to them.

The early IT outsourcing market grew rapidly but sometimes not as quickly as some of the service providers might have wished. During slack times some of the big providers took on clients that they would now consider too small. A couple of years ago EDS claimed to have a number of satisfied UK clients in the £10,000 a year range. Presumably, the contracts having been in existence for a long time and both EDS and their clients must find the arrangements profitable. Nevertheless, it is difficult to imagine that any of the larger providers would normally go out of their way to obtain a £10,000 per annum contract these days.

> most major providers break their own rules on minimum contract size when it suits them

'Normally' is the key word in the last statement because sometimes executives make decisions that they would not contemplate at other times. This frequently happens in the outsourcing market when sales are down because anticipated major wins have failed to materialize, key existing contracts have unexpectedly not been renewed or someone is tantalizingly close to an end of year sales target and a lucrative bonus. Rules, they say, are made to be broken and most major providers break their own rules on minimum contract size when it suits them.

Clearly, a large client organization will still be in a strong negotiating position even if it is outsourcing a small department. However, if a small or medium sized client with a relatively small area to outsource should be 'lucky' enough to sign a deal with a major provider because that provider has suddenly become desperate for an additional contract, the result will be difficult to forecast.

Hopefully, the provider will treat small clients as well as it does the large clients and new clients as well as it does existing clients. But resources are always scarce, so guess who usually gets priority if a specialist is urgently needed at both a large client's site and a small client's site? I accept that there might be exceptions to this natural law, but I doubt if there are many.

If the last twenty-odd years of outsourcing experience has taught us any lessons, then I suggest that the following are amongst the most important.

1 It is essential in an outsourcing arrangement that key elements such as the Service Level Agreements (SLAs) are adequately written up in the contract because they provide the legal structure by which the provider's performance can be measured. Nevertheless, even where the contract documentation has been found to be watertight from the client's point of view, there have still been numerous cases where the provider failed miserably to reach the desired targets.

2 Although some of these failures may have been due to simple incompetence, it has become apparent that the most common reason has been that at some stage the provider has become convinced that concentrating on other more lucrative contracts would produce a better return. Once that happens, it would appear that even the tightest of contracts can do little to safeguard the client's position.

3 For that reason, it is now believed that the wise client will build an element of risk/reward motivation into the arrangement so that there is always the opportunity that a special effort on the provider's part will produce an adequate reward.

4 Sadly, even these partnership arrangements have been known to fail and the reason put forward most often for this situation is that yet again the provider has found other, even more lucrative contracts.

The question of size is therefore very important. Apart from owning or taking an equity stake in the provider, the best thing a client can do when entering into an outsourcing arrangement is to ensure that the continuation of their arrangement is always going to be of prime importance to the provider. I appreciate that this is easier said than done, but clearly it is much more likely to be achieved if the client is a key player with a provider who has a small number of clients, than if it is a small player with a provider with many clients.

Different clients, different quality of service

I would doubt if any long-term outsourcing service provider could honestly claim that all its clients were satisfied with the service they have been receiving. But then again it would be surprising if any established supplier of products or services could make the claim – it is in the nature of commerce that you cannot satisfy everybody.

Nevertheless, some of the variations in performance by major outsourcing service providers have been most surprising when considered under normal business guidelines. Providers who have apparently produced excellent results for some clients in terms of service improvements and savings have followed this up with failures and then further successes and failures.

As the world's leading provider of IT and BPO services, it is worth looking at some of the deals EDS have been involved with. A few years ago they contracted to develop and build a Social Security system for the southern US State of Florida. Part-way through its first year of operation the system developed faults and then got progressively worse. The

State officials made the decision to stop paying EDS, who they held responsible for an unacceptable bottleneck in dealing with claims and for the system paying out over $100 million more than it should have done in benefits. EDS sued for non-payment, arguing that State officials had changed the system almost immediately it had been implemented and that as a result the amount of information that it needed to process was dramatically increased. More recently, EDS has provided more or less the same argument to explain why its outsourcing arrangement with the British Government's Child Support Agency ran into difficulties.

Politicians normally win office by promising changes and therefore, public sector outsourcing frequently carries the risk of disruption due to U-turns in policy. Nevertheless it is almost impossible to accurately apportion blame in these disputes because some changes to the required service are inevitable almost from the day the contract starts. From that point on even the most gifted arbitrator will find it difficult to estimate the extra degree of difficulty or disruption resulting from the change. EDS has a great deal of experience in dealing with the public sector. In recent years they have won contracts with a range of central government bodies in the UK, including the Inland Revenue, the CSA, the NHS, the Driver & Vehicle Licensing Agency, the DSS and a number of local authorities. EDS also provides similar services for government departments across North America and the Far East and has a similarly impressive list of private sector clients around the world. In fact, EDS has over 9000 clients on a global basis and they are the first choice of provider for many major clients, so they must be doing something right. Nevertheless, it would be unrealistic to expect every client to get the same quality of service, however hard EDS and other major service providers might try to achieve that aim.

> it would be unrealistic to expect every client to get the same quality of service, however hard EDS and other major service providers might try to achieve that aim

Getting involved in contract disputes can be a very expensive business, so it is normally true to say that few cases would end up in court if the result was a foregone conclusion, i.e. both parties must normally believe that they have a reasonable case for the dispute to get that far. Outsourcing disputes are no different from other contract disputes and decisions are sometimes in the balance until the very last minute. In fact, cynics will often argue that the decision would have different if another judge had made it, or the same judge had made it on a different day.

On balance, I think most outsourcing advisers would apportion most of the blame for the average failure with the client. The provider typically has the experience to avoid making too many mistakes but it's often all too new to the client and it is the client who usually introduces massive changes to procedures without having allowed for them in the contract.

Clearly, though, the service provider must be to blame for failure on some occasions, even though it may have been successful at around the same time for other clients. I believe, but I cannot prove it, that failure by one of these majors is most likely to happen because they have taken too much work on.

I accept that it would be difficult to know when a provider who already has thousands of clients is taking on too much work. Nevertheless, over the years I have noticed that when major consultancy firms first adopt a service provider role they tend to underestimate the amount of work that is involved. In addition they are always trying to come to terms with the fact that far more non-fee earning time is necessary in obtaining an outsourcing deal than is ever likely to happen in a conventional consultancy assignment.

This uncertainty has certainly led to some new service providers underestimating the time taken to pitch for new work in a competitive situation. In addition, of course, without previous experience they can sometimes only guess at the time and effort needed to bring about the transition, and if they get this horribly wrong there is a good chance it will never be put right. However, it goes much further than that. Even an experienced service provider can never be really certain how long the transition will take, as each new transition will not only contain unique elements but will be subject to varying degrees of helpfulness from the staff being transferred. The experienced service providers will probably be 10–15 per cent better in making such estimates but they can all get it wrong. Even the most experienced providers have known times when a major new client has been taken on just when problems have arisen unexpectedly with other existing clients' work. As a result there will be a great deal of stressful travelling around by key staff to correct the problem, but such a situation will not bode well for the new client's chance of getting good service at the first time of asking.

I think some service providers are never quite sure why one outsourcing project is an out and out success and another is a complete failure. Whilst I am sure that taking on too much work is a major reason and that a sudden increase in problems across existing clients is another, the human element must also be a major factor. Transferring IT, finance or any large function to a service provider is a major act of faith. So much of it depends on the management skills available to the project. The programme manager and other key members of the provider's staff may be experienced or inexperienced. They could be on the top of their form or suffering from depression or other illnesses. Similarly, the client's staff may be depressed or ill or just bloody-minded. In short, the difference between a very successful and an unsuccessful transition may simply be the atmosphere permeating around the management team or the fact that a key executive is ill.

in short, the difference between a very successful and an unsuccessful transition may simply be the atmosphere permeating around the management team or the fact that a key executive is ill

If I were contemplating outsourcing a major function, I would pay special attention to the people the provider was putting forward to run the project. Are they experienced in the roles they will be playing? If so, what success have they had? If not, can we afford to take the risk on this occasion? I would also examine the attitude of my own senior staff – those being transferred and those being retained. If these people were really negative it would be risky to let them play a key part in the transition.

On a regular basis throughout the transition I would make it my business to study the atmosphere being created by the interaction of the managers and at the first sign of problems I would demand changes.

chapter 7

the process of choosing a service provider

What are your main reasons for outsourcing?

One of the first tasks facing the management team of an organization embarking on an outsourcing project is to establish what it wants from the arrangement. These days most managers are familiar with the three basic reasons for outsourcing put forward by the management gurus:

- the desire to concentrate on core activities;

- the need to improve the service; and

- the often pressing need to reduce the cost.

Virtually all the initial approaches to service providers concentrate on these three points and consequently receive little attention unless the potential client explains them in a convincing way. More importantly, an assumption that the reasons are well known and obvious may mean that the client management has failed to analyze its own special reasons early enough.

Well before anything is sent to potential service providers, the client must establish what it really wants to achieve. Getting each of the senior managers of the function and the senior users to document their aims in order of priority is an excellent way of doing this. Even if a re-engineering exercise has recently been carried out, it still worth going through this exercise as it reinforces the question 'What are we trying to achieve by considering this option?'

It really is beneficial for the client's negotiators to be absolutely sure of the main reasons for considering outsourcing. If the key reason is to turn the service into something that better matches the perceived current and future needs of the users, then the negotiators are aware that a value added improved service is paramount and this could mean that the cost factor is significantly less important. It is conceivable that the comfort of knowing cost cutting is not the key aim may result in the opportunity for the service provider to maximize the client's competitiveness by creating a 'Rolls Royce' type service in the short term. Such an opportunity would certainly be lost if the service provider has any doubts about the client's main aims. These doubts arise automatically in outsourcing because any experienced service provider will have numerous stories to tell of potential clients who claimed that their main aim was an improved service and then chose the provider submitting the lowest cost without considering the service quality. In a competitive tendering situation, therefore, the provider usually starts by looking for ways to keep the costs as low as possible.

If a significantly improved service is paramount, it will be essential to stress this aim at every opportunity when writing to or talking to the competing providers in order to overcome any latent scepticism. However, emphasizing the need for an improved service need not reduce the opportunity for maximizing cost savings. A balance can be obtained by making it very clear that cost will only play a part in the decision should two providers submit equally attractive service proposals. All very obvious points, but it is surprising how often the client fails to communicate the real reasons for outsourcing to the service providers.

It is possible that after a stringent internal review, management will decide that cutting cost is really the only issue. Decisions of this type have sometimes been made where organizations anticipate major short-term acquisitions or divestments. They conclude, therefore, that it makes little sense building for the future if the future is too uncertain to even make a guess at. In addition, they reason, if disruption is the only certainty in the near future, an organization with more specialists and the opportunity to use them over a wide range of clients is bound to be able to perform the service more cost effectively. In such circumstances the client is looking for a service provider who will probably carry on the function without making too many changes but who can make savings from better use of personnel.

> outsourcing service providers invariably claim that their sole aim is to add value by using the latest technology to dramatically improve each client's service

Outsourcing service providers invariably claim that their sole aim is to add value by using the latest technology to dramatically improve each client's service. Nevertheless, for the vast majority of providers in functions like IT and finance, there will be many occasions when just taking over the service without the need to make significant changes will be a very attractive option. Clearly this will be the case where the provider is struggling to find the specialist resources to bring about improvements for other clients and where it sees the opportunity to share the new client's service with that provided for existing clients.

If the client is sure that its key reason for outsourcing is cost reduction then it will presumably want to limit the duration of the outsourcing contract. In such circumstances this ought to be made very clear to potential service providers from the beginning. In fact the fairest way for the client to deal with this type of arrangement is to provide a complete description of the function to be outsourced, including current costs, to a maximum of three service providers and see which one comes up with the best bid. Even then, the wise client will have made some preliminary overtures to establish a short list of potential service providers who are most likely to be attracted to such a deal at the time in question. A good way to establish this is to ask for permission to talk to some of their other local clients.

How do you find the right outsourcing service provider?

Use an ideal provider profile

First of all, it is essential for the client to draw up a profile of the ideal provider before contacting anyone. What type and range of specialist skills are necessary and in what quantity? If the provider experienced any shortfall in numbers and quality of specialists once the project was underway, would you be willing for sub-contractors to be used? Do you feel it is essential for the service provider of your non-core function to have worked for clients who are direct competitors in your core functions? In other words, is it important that they understand your business? What parameters do you wish to place on the size of potential service providers – does this refer to the total number of people they will put on your account or to the total number of staff they employ?

Invariably when you start to meet with potential service providers some of the parameters set will probably need to be adjusted, but it is still beneficial to do an ideal profiling exercise because it saves time and narrows the search. European public sector organizations are frequently forced to find outsourcing service providers by placing announcements inviting tenders in the *European Journal*. Even then it makes good sense to have completed this type of exercise before the potential providers respond.

For most private sector organizations it is a question of finding out who the most suitable providers are and then approaching one or more. These days it is easy to find relevant service providers. A few minutes on the internet should uncover more than you would ever want to talk to. Before you contact a service provider it is obviously desirable to get as much information about the company as you possibly can to compare with your ideal profile. This will take a little more time but the information necessary to narrow the search is likely to be found on the internet. Quite often the service providers' websites will contain snippets from articles they have featured in, statements regarding the areas they specialize in and, increasingly, case histories.

It is therefore possible to isolate a significant number of service providers in this way and many will appear to be a reasonable match with the ideal profile set. This is inevitable as most providers claim expertise over a wide range of activities.

Speak to existing clients

Other sections of this book deal with pros and cons of dealing with just one or multiples of providers. But, however many providers you contact, it is a good idea to ask each of them for permission to speak to at least one of their existing customers about the service they are currently receiving. Service providers don't enjoy being forced to make such introductions. Not all their clients will be happy with the service they are getting and there will be natural concern as to how many times you can keep bothering even the most satisfied of clients. Nevertheless, the service providers do accept that a potential client is contemplating a very risky venture over a relatively long period of time and is therefore justified in taking whatever steps it can to safeguard itself. Consequently, a good many potential clients do make these requests and the providers normally do their best to satisfy them.

Not surprisingly then, the service provider's 'flagship' clients often find themselves dealing with such enquiries on a very frequent basis. It is not unusual to find that these flagship clients are not necessary those receiving the best service, but the ones that have said the nicest things about the provider on previous occasions. In making such enquiries of an existing client it is well worth considering that the person you are talking to will normally be hoping for an ever improving service and will have few, if any, reasons for upsetting the provider, even if the service is not what is desired.

Armed with such knowledge, some potential clients have approached the flagship client with very detailed written questions aimed at forcing a truthful answer. In my experience this does not usually work, as the flagship client makes excuses about sudden pressures of work and resorts to very brief and vague answers.

It is usually better to adopt what will be seen as a softer approach. For example, if the first question is 'Has the service provider matched its promises and your expectations?' the person expected to answer is already under pressure and will probably immediately paint the provider's performance more favourably than was originally intended. After that, the person being questioned is very likely to go on giving the provider undue praise. On the other hand, if the first approach adopted the marketing intelligence reasoning by starting with a question such as 'What would you change if you had to do it all again?' the threat largely disappears. Answering this type of question does not necessarily imply criticism of the provider and consequently the interview gets off to a pleasant start and the potential client has the opportunity to learn much more about the provider's actual performance.

It will be particularly important to devise questions aimed at the provider's current workload. The provider may not have told the potential client that it has just won several major new contracts, which will all begin shortly, but that information will very likely have filtered through to the existing client's internal management from contacts with the provider. Contact with the service provider's existing clients is the best way to obtain information on the short- and medium-term suitability of potential providers.

> contact with the service provider's existing clients is the best way to obtain information on the short- and medium-term suitability of potential providers

How many providers should you approach?

For those clients intent on creating a competitive short list of service providers, the next question is: how many potential service providers is it right to deal with? Anyone who has set up such a competitive situation will confirm that dealing with three or four providers on a preliminary basis still involves a great deal of work, and that the workload for the client is only marginally reduced if client adviser consultants are involved. Incidentally, if it is intended to use such consultants then it is advisable to involve them before any contact is made with providers, as they may have valuable information on the short-term circumstances affecting one or more of the providers.

In most circumstances, two to three short-listed providers will be sufficient for any client's needs, but this will depend to a large extent on the quality of the refining process used to create the short list.

Developing the partnership concept

Once the successful service provider has been chosen, the two parties will want to firm up the basis on which they are going to work together. Invariably these days one or other party will raise the subject of a partnership of some type early in the discussions.

It is worth setting down what the partnership concept means in the outsourcing environment where a specific joint venture is not contemplated.

- Both parties accept that a rigid contract would be too restrictive in their future relationship because they want to be flexible enough to maximize the opportunities that appear to exist. In effect they have identified in non-specific terms what they want to achieve but accept that the means of reaching the targets are not yet fully understood and in any case can only be reached over a period of time.

- That does not mean that a contract is not necessary at all. It is important that the original intent of the partnership is written down so that any key relevant individual can refer to it whenever this becomes necessary.

- In fact, a conventional contract is often used for partnership agreements, but is amended in areas that stipulate performance. For example, the service level agreement could still be included as a target to be reached or bettered. In the partnership agreement though, the typical minimum performance level might not be mentioned and could be replaced by a clause that simply urged both parties to do their best to achieve the desired results.

- Usually, a separate document is attached or included in the contract specifying both parties' responsibilities in achieving the set aims.

- The partnership contract or agreement must spell out the targets that both parties have set whilst allowing flexibility for the provider to try alternative ways of reaching the desired goals.

Staff issues

When should you inform your staff of the potential outsourcing?

The usual answer to this question is to make the announcement as soon as you possibly can. Nevertheless, some common sense must be applied.

The process of outsourcing complex non-core functions like IT and finance can take a very long time. The time taken from outsourcing first being considered as a serious option to the actual transfer date has been known to take a year or so, with the average being at least six months. These days at least 90 per cent of organizations which decide that outsourcing is the preferred option for IT, will outsource the function within a nine to eighteen month period. With other functions like finance and HR there is a greater chance that the client management will change its mind at some stage prior to signing a contract.

In circumstances where the process is likely to take many months and is by no means certain to result in an outsourcing, the subject of when to inform the staff likely to be transferred is worthy of considerable thought. Although it may be morally correct for an organization to inform its employees of major lifestyle changes as soon as it is aware of them, this ought to be balanced against the uncertainty and dissatisfaction that a long period of waiting will create in the mind of the average employee.

> although it may be morally correct for an organization to inform its employees of major lifestyle changes as soon as it is aware of them, this ought to be balanced against the uncertainty and dissatisfaction that a long period of waiting will create in the mind of the average employee

Those in favour of giving as much notice as possible will quote instances where junior staff have not been told that an outsourcing project was in progress and unfortunately made decisions to buy local property. Obviously anyone taking such a decision only to find that within months they had to relocate if they wanted to keep their job is likely to be upset. Those against, point to instances where all staff were told of the outsourcing possibility almost as soon as this option was first considered, but because it took many months to choose the provider a great many of them took the opportunity to change jobs. Once the outsourcing option is raised, the identity, management and management style of the successful service provider is going to assume great importance to the functions employees. It follows, then, that as soon as the successful service provider is known, its management should be introduced to the client's staff to allay their fears as quickly as possible.

Sometimes it is deemed necessary for the provider's consultants to visit the client's premises in order to carry out some work that is essential to the outsourcing proceeding. The presence of a service provider's consultants on the client's premises might be disguised in the first instance as a normal consultancy assignment but it would add to any feelings of betrayal if it later became obvious that the consultancy had been the start of the outsourcing exercise.

Logically, then, in most instances it makes sense not to inform the staff likely to be transferred until a preferred supplier has been chosen. If a competitive situation between service providers exists for any length of time and the client needs to allow access to senior staff in order to enhance this competition, then it is important that these meetings take place off-site.

The importance of prompt briefing and comforting of staff

From the moment that outsourcing becomes the preferred option, the client should immediately start working on the detail necessary to inform the staff and bring about a smooth transition. In this the client can and should look for assistance from the short-listed providers because previous experience of transitions will be invaluable.

In any outsourcing, the main factor in securing a successful service delivery will be the attitude of the staff, both those retained and those to be transferred. It is, therefore, important to maintain goodwill between the two groups of staff and reduce the worry and uncertainty time to an absolute minimum. Whatever efforts are made to inform and comfort those concerned, strong feelings of resentment and betrayal will linger with all staff, particularly those who are being made redundant, unless something special is done to compensate.

It is extremely important not just to inform the employees, but to treat and help them to an extent that has probably not been deemed necessary before. Looking at it purely from the client's and provider's points of view, it is of paramount importance to provide first rate assistance to any staff who are immediately being made redundant. Ignoring the moral grounds for treating staff well, it is essential to be seen to be concerned, both because the people being transferred may judge their own future treatment on what they see and hear during this time, and because some of those being made redundant may be required to work on during the transition period on a contract or incentive basis.

Given the tension that the employees will experience it is advisable at least to consider the following steps and actions.

1   The client should outline its own strategy from the time outsourcing becomes the preferred option. 'How would I both expect and wish to be treated?' is a good starting point.

2   The client and successful provider must agree a strategy for dealing with the staff, particularly those who will be transferred, and this will ideally be done prior to the announcement.

3   It is important for the successful provider to meet with the client's human resource management to understand the issues that will need to be addressed quickly in respect of group and individual terms and conditions, trade union involvement, etc.

4   It will be important to bring together all the necessary information to be able to agree each individual's future terms and conditions as soon as possible to avoid unnecessary arguments later.

5   As soon as the initial announcement has been made, firm dates should be given to each affected employee as to when they will receive one to one and probably group opportunities to communicate with representatives of both existing and future employers. These meetings should be carried out as quickly as possible.

6   The period immediately following the announcement will be an uncomfortable and traumatic time for the employees and it is likely that each person to be transferred will initially seek to direct most questions at their existing management, but gradually they will become more interested in talking to their future employers. In order to answer employees' questions to the satisfaction of all concerned, it will be desirable for the provider's representatives to be aware of sensitive information such as terms and employment conditions, even though the contract will not be in place.

7   In view of the emotional stress likely in the short term, both parties must make themselves available whenever possible, and commit as much information as possible to writing so that unnecessary problems do not arise. For example, after the announcement of an impending outsourcing, rumours often start to spread that a relocation or further relocation will be required in the short term. Therefore, if this is not contemplated, it would be advisable to counter any possible concerns by the provider putting in writing its intentions regarding the location issue.

8   Most of the large service providers claim that they view their initial contact with their new employees with such concern that they use well trained and

sensitive human resource specialists in these first interviews, which are treated as counselling sessions. The concerned client would be advised to get an early indication of exactly what the provider is going to do in this area.

9 Most providers will wish to introduce their own general terms and conditions of employment into the discussions as early as practicable in these initial counselling sessions. Experience indicates that the sooner this area of uncertainty is removed, the better the employees' reaction will be. However, the service provider may not wish to finalize individual terms during a first meeting. This may be due to uncertainty about the individual, or the group terms may not have been finalized. The client should either 'sit in' on the provider's discussions with staff to be transferred, or counsel selected members of the staff immediately after they have been involved in one to one sessions with the provider. If the client feels that the provider has not done enough to allay unnecessary fears then it should push for additional action on this point to be taken as quickly as possible. Client management should be aware that they are likely to be blamed for all problems that occur prior to the transition being completed. After all, they decided to outsource.

10 In further (probably group) sessions, the provider will wish to go into more detail regarding initial induction training (to explain operating systems and working practices), further individual and group training plans, career development and personnel policies. Again, it is in the client's interest to make sure all these actions take place.

A first class service provider's overall aims during these initial contacts will include:

● gaining an understanding of each individual's personal aims and aspirations and the 'culture' they will be moving from in order to minimize the prospect of these issues being badly handled and resulting in a reduced service;

● creating the impression that by moving to the new organization, the employees' skills, experience and expertise are more closely related to the core activities than was previously the case, and that consequently opportunities for career development and enhancement will be markedly increased;

● the settlement of all employee matters as quickly as possible, particularly with the managers who will be transferring, as they will have a key role to play if the new service is to meet expectations; and

● creating an atmosphere whereby the transferred staff are pleased that the transfer is about to take place and are looking forward to this new stage in their careers.

> the important thing to remember is that despite the very best intentions and support from senior management, the outsourcing will not be a success if there is not a reasonable degree of support from the staff

The important thing to remember is that despite the very best intentions and support from senior management, the outsourcing will not be a success if there is not a reasonable degree of support from the staff. It will be important to communicate the benefits of outsourcing from both the organization's and the employees' point of view. One further point is worth making on the subject of counselling staff. Some client organizations have been known to stress the benefits of outsourcing too strongly, with the result that staff the client intended to retain in house have 'jumped ship' either to the provider or some third party.

Should you allow the internal staff to make a competitive bid?

Clearly, if an internal team is going to be allowed to bid then they should probably be given some advance notice to compensate for the lack of experience in mounting such competitive bids. However, it should not be too advanced, as there is a chance that the time will be used to block the competition and the external providers must feel that they have a reasonable chance of success. Apart from this extra time, it is essential that as far as possible, all bidders believe they are performing on a reasonably level playing field.

Finding a suitable provider by sole sourcing

The number of outsourcing deals that have been put together as a result of single tender or sole sourcing arrangements is variously estimated to be anywhere between 25 and 60 per cent of the total for all deals. Whatever the true figure, it is, on the face of it, quite extraordinary that any client organization should not bother to take advantage of competitive advice, ideas and quotations when making a very important outsourcing decision.

A number of service providers and consultancies such as Unisys, argue that sole sourcing is good for the client and give reasons such as the following.

● Saving time and money are two of the main motives for outsourcing, and when a customer selects a single vendor to perform a service instead of going out to competitive bid, even more time and money is saved.

● Sole sourcing can increase the control an organization has over the outsourcing process and adds value to the situation.

● Sole sourcing shortens the procurement cycle.

●   Sole sourcing reduces procurement cycle costs.

●   The alternative request for proposal (RFP) process has become extremely costly and time consuming.

Without doubt, there are organizations whose need to outsource is so pressing that they probably do need to avoid the time taken in setting up a competitive situation. It is equally true that the time taken to organize a competitive base via a RFP is normally much too long and is frequently ludicrously expensive. However, advocates of full competition will justifiably argue that the client organization is going to get much more control over the outsourcing process by creating a competition. They will also be quick to point out that sole sourcing runs the risk that there is no obvious second provider to fall back on if the deal with the first choice company falls through.

It may be that some client organizations have made a deliberate decision to save time and cost by going the sole sourcing route. In most cases, though, sole sourcing appears to happen from a variety of 'accidents'.

Usual reasons why sole sourcing takes place

Once outsourcing has been accepted as a serious method of improving performance, the client's management team must work out how best to investigate this option and they must do so in circumstances requiring a high level of security. In all probability they will deem it an essential first step to talk to at least one trustworthy individual who can shed some light on the subject.

> once outsourcing has been accepted as a serious method of improving performance, the client's management team must work out how best to investigate this option and they must do so in circumstances requiring a high level of security

The auditor's involvement

Quite naturally, many organizations have approached the contact partner at their auditors to fill this role. Apart from knowing the client's business very well, an audit partner may be working for a firm that is a potential service provider or supplies outsourcing consultancy advice. If the auditing firm does provide either of these services, the client may hope that they can gain access to valuable information without divulging their identity.

In making this assumption, client management will have reasoned that the partner concerned will not want to lose the audit and will therefore not risk directly involving any other part of the firm until the client gives permission to do so. In addition, knowledge that the auditing firm cannot be both auditor and service provider for the finance function may have convinced some managers that an approach to the audit partner will be totally risk free.

Whatever the logic behind the approach, a significant number of outsourcing arrangements for both IT and finance have started with the introduction of the audit partner, and some of them have become sole sourcing deals with other parts of the partner's firm. There is no suggestion of wrongdoing here. Few audit partners will want to lose an important audit, but once a partner has exhausted his or her pot of knowledge, it is natural for that partner to point out that experts exist in other parts of the firm. A meeting of interested parties is arranged, after which, events take their natural course.

From the major accountancy-based firms' point of view, the potential rewards from being an outsourcing service provider are massive for both IT and finance when compared to what can be obtained from auditing. For that reason, many of these firms have already taken a decision at the highest level to give up the audit if necessary, if an outsourcing opportunity should arise.

An organization that begins sole sourcing discussions with its audit firm prior to talking to anyone else can put itself at a disadvantage, even where the finance function is not a candidate for initial outsourcing. The potential client must accept that it will be difficult for any other bidders to be equally briefed without going to a great deal of effort and without passing out even more sensitive information than would otherwise be necessary. The client may be prepared to do this, or may decide that it does not matter if the audit firm does have more information than the other potential service providers. Unfortunately and for obvious reasons, the other service providers will see themselves at a considerable disadvantage in this arrangement.

Approaching just one service provider

Many organizations contemplating outsourcing a major function take 'the bull by the horns' and as a first step, contact what they take to be the most likely service provider. Naturally, they explain that, as yet, outsourcing is just one of many options and in order to take the matter further they would like to know what information the provider needs in order to put a price on meeting a specified service level. The provider reacts by stating that it would need to understand not only the transaction details but also how the various processes fit into the client's overall strategy and the real level of service that is required for the medium and long term. The provider will argue, with every justification, that this is best done by a series of exploratory meetings with the senior and middle managers, during which time the detail necessary to make a bid will be extracted.

In many sole sourcing arrangements the client's original idea behind talking to the service provider was to obtain the basic information necessary to produce a Request for Proposal (RFP). The provider's insistence that it will be necessary to talk at length with the client's middle management before any meaningful estimate of service and costs could be made, appears to have typically resulted in the following line of thought.

- We know our business is complex, therefore this service provider is correct, it will obviously need time studying transaction details and talking to our staff – we could not expect it or any other provider to make a bid based simply on an RFP.

- Ideally, we do not want to give sensitive information of this type to any outside organization, so we certainly must not give it to more than one.

- If we give the service provider the amount of detail necessary to make a sensible bid, how can we do it without also giving it a good idea of what the service currently costs?

- If we cannot disguise what the current service costs are, then that surely removes much of the reason for trying to create a competition.

- We want to delay upsetting the staff for as long as possible, why create a long period of unrest for nothing if we eventually decide not to outsource. We can, therefore, really only achieve our aim of pursuing the outsourcing option but not upsetting the staff by dealing with one provider on a very careful step-by-step basis.

Every organization contemplating outsourcing should accept that it starts from a disadvantageous position when compared to the service providers it will be negotiating with. Even if it has previous outsourcing experience available, it may not have outsourced the function in question before. Compared to that, the service provider will have a great deal of information on what constitutes best practice for that function.

A service provider that has been operating for a number of years may have worked with hundreds of clients carrying out the same function. Inevitably each new assignment adds to the collective wisdom of the provider. In addition, the top providers will seek out best practice information on a regular basis by way of benchmarking and other exercises. In this way they will almost always be able to find existing 'evidence' allowing them to make an indicative bid, based almost entirely on the potential client's transaction information.

> every organization contemplating outsourcing should accept that it starts from a disadvantageous position when compared to the service providers it will be negotiating with

Not having the same level of best practice information means that the client organization will not be able to estimate the real value of a bid made on a sole sourcing basis. If such a bid offers the client a 20 per cent saving, it may disguise the fact that the provider is able to provide the service at less than half the client's current cost and is making a substantial profit. In a competitive situation, a serious bidder could not be certain of the level of other bids and consequently would be inclined to keep the price as low as possible. It is likely, therefore, that the client would have obtained significantly greater savings from a competitive situation.

Organizations start from a similarly disadvantaged position in all commercial dealings with specialist suppliers, but overcome this situation by creating competition for the work to be carried out. The problem with outsourcing is that it appears to be very difficult to create the necessary competition without risking staff disruption and giving too many people sensitive information.

Other reasons for taking the sole sourcing route

Some substantial outsourcing arrangements have started on a small scale, possibly with an IT facilities management contract and then graduated to a full outsourcing as a natural result of the provider doing a good job.

Other outsourcings have resulted from consultancy assignments where because the consultant's people detailed the advantages and the path to follow to outsourcing, and because the consultancy was also an outsourcing service provider, it appeared neither fair nor logical to involve competitors. This has been particularly true where the opportunity for a joint venture between the two parties has been isolated.

Many organizations that have chosen the sole sourcing route will nevertheless claim that they had gone through a competitive process by asking a number of service providers to make general presentations. However, a 'beauty parade' of service providers which does not result in competitive bids because the client is reluctant to give all the service providers the necessary information, cannot really create the correct level of competition.

Some organizations have confused themselves by believing that because they find the function difficult to bring under control, then it must be too complex to explain in an RFP. The irony is that the service providers usually only require the most basic of transaction details in order to submit a bid, because they base their calculations on best practice and their own past experience of what is involved in the client's transactions and processes.

The service provider obtains many advantages from being chosen in a sole sourcing arrangement, including saving the significant costs involved in a competition. The benefits are such that given any opportunity for a non-competitive business deal, the provider will make every effort and excuse to get in quickly to talk to the potential client's staff. They know that if they get in and are able to stay in for any length of time, the less likely it is that the client will want to go through the same exercise with anyone else.

Sometimes the client's management starts off with a great deal of faith in one provider and readily adopts the view that they either outsource to this provider or they don't outsource at all. However, even then they should not discard the competitive process altogether because they may be approaching this ideal provider at a point in time when it has little or no reason to offer anything but the smallest margin. This can happen when they have a surfeit of work in the outsourcing area or where they are under extreme pressure to meet targets for other clients.

However logical the sole sourcing approach may appear at the time, there must be a risk that the client finishes up paying a higher price than it would have done if it had created real competition.

> however logical the sole sourcing approach may appear at the time, there must be a risk that the client finishes up paying a higher price than it would have done if it had created real competition

The client may not have told the provider what the service was currently costing and did not provide any information on staffing levels. The client may hope that as a result the provider will have to keep its price as low as possible to be sure of offering an improvement on the current situation. There are two main snags with this reasoning. The first is that, once two or three of the client's middle management have been interviewed for as little as 15 minutes, there is a very strong chance that the provider will have a good idea of the staffing levels, even though no individual manager will remember giving anything away. The second is that the provider will make its own estimates based on best practice information and will still do so even if it has been given the costs and staffing levels to start off with.

Once the provider has studied the client's transaction details plus any reporting analysis work that is also part of the arrangement, it will compare this against what it believes is possible after it has re-engineered the service and has completed any other necessary changes. Typically, it will separate the cost of new systems and other transition costs for these to be paid when necessary by the client. It could be argued that these transition costs would most likely be lower if real competition played a part.

The share of the anticipated savings that the providers offer the client will depend on a number of factors, including how important they value the client in question, how much they need the work and has competitive the situation is. For that reason a client who only deals with one provider is unlikely to save as much as one who has created real competition amongst several providers. If, for example, the provider not facing competition can see that costs have been outstripping inflation and then is able to get confirmation that this factor is the main reason for outsourcing, there is no reason to offer a competitive price. It may be sufficient, in terms of winning the business, to offer a constant price for each of, say, five years at more or less the client's current cost level.

Using more than one provider

There has been a steadily increasing trend amongst major client organizations to split the overall IT function into sub-functions that can be operated and managed separately by outsourcing service providers. The stated objective of some of these organizations is to obtain the best specialist suppliers for each sub-function. Others have taken this route for defensive reasons, which include not committing everything to one external supplier and the belief that outsourcing in this way makes it easier to take the service back in house should it become necessary. From a contractual point of view it is certainly possible to get just as good an exit strategy built into an arrangement with one provider as it is with many. Nevertheless, for most executives, it still 'feels' easier to consider exiting if the IT outsourcing arrangement has been split up.

I know of no hard evidence in terms of service benefits or cost savings, in favour of using either a single provider or multiples of providers. The evidence probably already exists but it's certainly not surfaced for reasoned examination so far. As yet, the single versus several providers question has been mainly confined to IT outsourcing and will probably be confined to that function. It will probably also be confined to the very large clients because the service providers will not go to the trouble of co-operating with other providers if the deal and prestige factors are less than top drawer.

Logically, clients outsourcing only a portion of the IT infrastructure, e.g. desktops, will only use a single provider. If the outsourcing arrangement includes a range of components that are capable of being managed and operated separately, e.g. desktop, helpdesk and data-centre, then the multiple provider approach has more credibility.

Those in favour of multiple supplier deals will often point to the increased chance of getting real specialists working in each key area. Those against argue that splitting the function into two or more parts is bound to reduce the service level and savings obtained because each individual contract is that much less attractive to the providers.

Managing more than one provider

There is also the key question of how you manage the arrangement. In its much publicised mid 1990s IT outsourcing, BP Exploration claimed to have solved this problem by appointing three specialists on a worldwide basis, with each provider looking after the same specialist area all over the globe. In addition, however, the BP Exploration world of operations was split into three groups: North America, Europe and the rest of the world and each of the three providers was given control of the operation in one group. In that area the provider was made totally responsible to BP Exploration for the performance of the other two providers. Obviously, an arrangement of this type will necessitate the existence of a prime contract and very clearly defined sub-contracts.

Unless the client makes one service provider responsible for all the IT activities in one group or at one site, it will need to create a set of separate contracts and some form of co-operation agreement between itself and all the relevant service providers. Clearly, the advantages of making one provider responsible for the service normally outweigh the disadvantages. Having to negotiate with several providers to solve a problem will be difficult if there is any chance of the providers being able to transfer blame to others. It is sometimes argued that in law putting one provider in overall control will limit the client's ability to deal on a day-to-day basis with the other providers. But in practice it is a relatively simple task for the client to build this requirement into the contract.

The main provider will obviously take on the difficult task of managing the other providers on the site. This will have to be paid for as an extra in the contract but it could be argued that this fee will probably be less than the cost the client would incur trying to manage all the providers separately itself.

However, even where one provider has ultimate responsibility for the actions of other providers and minor sub-contractors on a site, it would be very unwise for the client to 'leave them to get on with it'. A client that has based its choice of providers on the 'best of breed' basis will need to consider other factors before it can hope to achieve its aims. For a start, service providers will not be overjoyed at the prospect of working closely with competitors. You may have chosen the providers on a 'best of breed' basis but the likelihood is that all the providers will supply the full range of IT services for other clients. They will also see themselves competing in the future for both full and part IT outsourcings. Not an ideal basis on which to expect them to co-operate fully and swap sensitive information.

> even where one provider has ultimate responsibility for the actions of other providers and minor sub-contractors on a site, it would be very unwise for the client to 'leave them to get on with it'

If the PR handouts are to be believed, then there is some evidence that a prime service provider can manage the day-to-day running of a multiple provider operation perfectly adequately and cost effectively for the client. Nevertheless, if the system fails, the client had better be prepared to find out the source of the problem by itself. Was it really a software problem or was it something else? Then, when the guilty provider is found, how do you compensate the others? Should you compensate the others?

Given all the various possibilities it would appear likely that for a very large client there may be initial cost benefits in the 'best of breed' approach, i.e. the overall cost of the total IT outsourcing may be less if it is split up in this way. Nevertheless, I would expect that in the majority of cases and over time the cost of managing inter-provider disputes is likely to outweigh the initial cost advantages.

One thing is certain – appointing a prime service provider to manage the activities of other providers may sometimes work well on a day-to-day basis, but it removes none of the client's need to manage the overall function – if anything it may require more management activity.

Pre-contract work

It is not unusual for the provider to suggest some pre-contract work. Cynics would argue that providers have two very good reasons for making such a suggestion. These are that the exercise will provide consultancy fee income; and that the presence of the provider in the client's premises will minimize the chance of a competitor getting in, even if both parties are keen to disguise the fact that the work is associated with outsourcing.

It follows then that in most instances it would be wise for the client not to agree to such work until its management has decided upon its chosen service provider.

Pre-contract consultancy can sometimes be justified where the client is very concerned about the risks involved. In such circumstances the client's senior management may feel that any additional cost (for much of the work would need to be done anyway if the contract goes ahead) is well justified.

If pre-contract consultancy is agreed upon, then typically, it will cover:

- the documentation of existing systems at all relevant sites in order to confirm the final design of systems for the outsourced services;

- a risk assessment to identify major areas of potential failure or delay in both service delivery and any new systems implementation contemplated; and

- the production of detailed specifications for each function to be transferred and, if relevant, a detailed systems implementation plan.

Some things a provider needs to know

Experience suggests that outsourcing service providers often fail to understand what potential clients are looking for when they originally begin a search for a provider. In particular, they fail to understand that the client will probably be looking for different things at different times in the negotiations. For example, when first creating a short list of potential providers, the client will probably consider the following factors in descending order of priority.

1. *Credibility* – how much experience does the provider have, i.e. how many existing clients?

2. *Reliability* – does the provider satisfy its clients' needs?

3. *Flexibility* – does the provider work to only one set work pattern, or is it flexible enough to match our needs in the short term and adjust further if our business grows substantially, or declines?

4. *Skill base* – does the provider have the IT and other skills that we may not need now but probably will later?

5. *Potential savings* – will this provider be able to offer greater or lesser savings than others?

6. *Service* – how will this provider's service compare with what we currently enjoy or what others might provide?

7. *Management skills* – if our business grows or contracts, does the provider have the management time, skills and desire to support our needs?

8. *Personnel policy* – what is the provider's personnel policy and how will this affect our people?

9. *Transition skills* – how effective have they been in bringing about past transitions: have they met the required timescales and what has been the effect on previously transferred staff?

10. *Contract questions* – will the provider want to use its greater experience and tie us down under a tight contract, or will it allow us a 'get out clause' or partnership arrangement?

11. *In-house expertise and control* – will the provider make sure that we do not lose the expertise and control necessary to maintain and develop the business?

It could be argued that the above list is in the wrong order, i.e. that the service is the most important issue, followed by the potential savings, etc. Indeed, in the final stages of most negotiations these are the issues on which the decision is normally based. However, in the very early stages of choosing potential providers it is usually only the first four 'concerns' that are important. In other words, it is only the client's perceived impression of the potential provider's credibility, reliability, flexibility and skill base that decides whether that provider gets to the negotiating table. Once the short-list stage is reached, though, these four factors are usually taken for granted and consequently play a less important part in the final decision.

Credibility, reliability and the skill base are factors that the service provider either has or does not have in the required amounts. It is normally sufficient, therefore, for the service provider to understand their special importance in the early stages of negotiations and to adjust its marketing accordingly. The flexibility factor is worth expanding a little further. The short-term flexibility concerns for most clients are based on issues such as:

- we are not sure whether it is in our best interest for the work to be done in the existing premises or for it to be done elsewhere;

- we are not sure whether we will ask the service provider to keep at the end of the transition, 100, 50 or 0 per cent of the staff currently employed;

- we will probably want to retain the existing systems, but then again, we might ask the provider to transfer them to its own systems or create new systems.

It is not unusual for potential clients to request this level of flexibility in the early stages. In one case, a provider refused very early on to say that it would retain all the staff who wanted to be transferred for at least six months after the transition. This refusal was a factor in the provider being dropped from the short list, but the remaining provider managed, without too much trouble, to make 20 per cent of the client's staff redundant by the end of the transition.

Naturally, the more flexible you are, the less profit you make. However, the point I am trying to make here is that flexibility is usually very important to the client during the initial discussions and very often the provider fails to pick up the emotional signals being generated. It is wise to state that 'all these solutions are possible' unless, of course, they are not. One major supplier claims total flexibility but usually all their clients get offered more or less the same package in the early stages. If a service provider is prepared to be as flexible as possible then it would be wise to raise this issue with the potential client at a very early stage.

chapter

potential drivers of outsourcing

Improved cash-flow

Sometimes the service provider will be obliged to pay for assets that are transferred from the client. Payments have frequently been made to cover property, computer hardware and other related equipment, software licences and transport. The logic behind this arrangement is that the provider then uses these assets to provide the agreed or part of the agreed service. Less frequently payment has been made (usually quite small) for items appearing under headings such as 'Goodwill'. Typically this occurs when the provider takes the asset but has little or no use for it. In effect both parties accept that new improved assets will be necessary very early on in the arrangement.

In some outsourcing arrangements an injection of cash is just another benefit to the client. In others, however, the outsourcing deal appears to have mainly come about because of the client's need for new short-term funds.

The need to relocate

A primary driver for many early IT outsourcing deals has been the need to relocate. For many organizations the 1980s was a time when internal IT departments grew rapidly. Very often these IT departments grew at a much greater rate than all the other functions in terms of employees and demands on resources.

> a primary driver for many early IT outsourcing deals has been the need to relocate

When the time came to seek out new premises, the senior IT executives often found it difficult to justify their excessive use of scarce resources and were frequently unconvincing in their estimates of future requirements. Given such circumstances it is not surprising that management sometimes took the safe way out and outsourced.

Non-competitive systems

During the latter part of the 1990s, the single most important reason why organizations began to consider outsourcing the finance function was the impending need to change the financial system. When the heavy cost of such an implementation is added to the disruption caused, it tends to concentrate the corporate mind. Analysis of past lack of success in financial system implementations was then sufficient reason to consider alternatives.

Knowledge that some outsourcing service providers have made substantial investments in the necessary technology and can claim extensive recent implementation experience with relevant systems is normally sufficient to spark the initial interest. Typically the client organization attempts to cost out the various options open to it under headings such as:

- do the implementation work ourselves with just the help of the successful software vendor's people;

- as above but use additional consultants;

- just outsource the creation and implementation of the new system to either a consultancy or an outsourcing service provider, i.e. indulge in 'Transformational Outsourcing'. This assumes that the client's staff would continue with their existing tasks, leaving the third party to develop the new system, largely to their own design. On completion, the new system is simply taken over by the existing staff. At no stage is there a transfer of employment;

- begin a full outsourcing arrangement.

Consolidate the latest improvements

Whatever the perceived level of success, the completion of a performance improvement project will normally mean that the function concerned is very unlikely to be considered a prime target for outsourcing in the short term. However, a number of enlightened organizations have taken the opposite view. Their reasoning is as follows.

- What we have just achieved is the best we can do. Therefore it is the right time to consider outsourcing, as we know what it costs us to provide a given level of service now.

- By outsourcing now we will not be giving the service provider easy savings.

- We are unlikely to keep this function continually up to date and therefore in perhaps just a few short months the systems will become less efficient and less productive.

- If we can find a world class provider, now is the right time to consider outsourcing.

Release scarce resources for other areas of business

Competition, market changes and ever changing technologies have caused many functional heads and their senior staff to be almost permanently engaged on so-called 'fire fighting' exercises. In theory, outsourcing should free much of this management time for more creative work.

Strategic reasons

Some organizations have made the strategic decision to concentrate all or most of the resources available on core functions. In such circumstances outsourcing becomes almost inevitable. Outsourcing allows an organization to focus on its core business by transferring operational functions to an external specialist.

> outsourcing allows an organization to focus on its core business by transferring operational functions to an external specialist

Risk reduction

The accelerating rate of change means that each and every investment an organization makes becomes ever more risky. Competitive activity, technology and legislation can all change overnight.

The outsourcing service provider is subject to the same risk but this can be significantly reduced when the investment is made for and spread over the work carried out for a range of clients.

Outsourcing can produce its own unique risks. Nike, the owner of the sports shoe brand, developed a strategy for outsourcing the manufacture of its shoes. Over a period of time, more and more production was centred on plants in Asia. After the usual initial teething troubles, they started to get satisfactory product at a relatively low cost.

Then Nike started to get a bad press because of alleged 'sweatshop' conditions in some of the Asian plants. The company was eventually compelled to cancel contracts with four factories in Indonesia. The reasons given for these cancellations included paying lower wages and providing poorer working conditions than the agreements stipulated.

This illustrates the need in all outsourcing arrangements for the client to make sure it fully understands what the service provider is, or is not, doing. In many cases insisting on regular access to all the provider's relevant sites is the only way to achieve this aim.

chapter 9

risks and concerns for both parties

The client's perceived risks

During the early outsourcing discussions it is only natural for the client's management to have serious doubts about the desirability of transferring key business areas to a third party. Some of these doubts will be viewed as real risk areas, others will be seen as relatively vague concerns that may or may not come to represent a real problem.

What do we do if we want to take the service back?

The answer, as far as there can be an answer, is to build an exit strategy into the contract. The exit terms open to the client will depend to a very large extent on its own negotiating power and how keen the service provider is to secure the business.

Any worthwhile exit strategy will need to put the client back in a position to carry on the business without disruption. Therefore, if the people, equipment and property have been transferred then the exit strategy should either allow for them to be transferred back or alternative arrangements made. Both parties need to be particularly careful where property is being transferred if the provider is intent on using the site for other clients' business. It is also worth stating that even where the contract allows for the return of the staff, the chances are that they would prefer to remain with the provider and as a result some disruption might result.

> any worthwhile exit strategy will need to put the client back in a position to carry on the business without disruption

What happens if the service provider is taken over or merges with another company or goes bust?

Any client organization considering outsourcing its finance and accountancy to a member of the Big Five must give this matter serious consideration. No one expected that the recent merger between Price Waterhouse and Coopers & Lybrand that formed PricewaterhouseCoopers was going to be the last example of consolidation between this group of large firms. But few outsiders really expected the sale of Ernst & Young's consultancy division to Cap Gemini to take place and at the time of writing several others of these large firms are considering splitting off their consultancy operations.

We used to argue that the worst scenario in outsourcing finance would occur when the client's service provider merged with their audit firm. In this eventuality the client would either have to find a new service provider or a new auditor and for reasons stated elsewhere, it is reasonable to expect the accountancy firm to offer to give up the audit in such circumstances. However, if the Ernst & Young example becomes the norm, then this potential problem would disappear because it is invariably the consultancy divisions of these large firms than provide the financial outsourcing services.

The major IT service providers such as EDS and CSC are all growing quickly and many have been in acquisitive mode in recent times, particularly in buying firms of consultants. In the circumstances it would be surprising if further mergers and acquisitions involving them did not take place in the near future. Generally speaking, the outsourcing market has been as prone to mergers and acquisitions as any other industry and one must expect some more activity as potential providers seek opportunities for growth.

A service provider involved in such a merger will need to make extra efforts to ensure that the service level is maintained and communication with the client treated as a major priority. However, a merger or acquisition is not predestined to seriously affect the relationship because in all probability the same people on the client's side will still be dealing with the same people on the provider's side and most of these are likely to have transferred from the client.

Not all service providers are blessed with top quality management and they are not immune from the range of problems facing other types of businesses, such as making bad decisions or enduring bad luck. Service providers can, therefore, collapse leaving their clients in trouble. It is to be hoped that, in most cases another provider will step in quickly to pick up the pieces. Nevertheless, the clients are always going to suffer in such circumstances and this factor alone justifies the careful study of providers even before they are short-listed.

Will the service be flexible enough to cater for major changes?

The addition or loss of business due to acquiring or selling divisions or whole companies will usually require a great deal of extra effort and creativity to manage whether the service is outsourced or not. In the traditional business environment the future uncertainty of such changes to workload is such that planning for their eventuality is largely ignored.

In an outsourced situation, however, the client can request that unexpected business demands be allowed for. For example, it might be written into the contract that the agreed service level would be maintained and charged for at a proportionate rate, even if the workload increased or decreased by say 20 per cent. The necessary terms to ensure that this happens will need to be spelt out in the contract. In addition the spirit behind this approach should be written down and form part of the management culture.

It may appear unfair that allowing for these unexpected business demands should form part of a contract when the client would not be in a position to obtain the same benefits if the service was to remain in house. However, the service provider will be in a completely different situation as regards potential business growth. This will be particularly true if the provider can see the service growing on the site from other developments with other clients.

Disrupting business during the transition to the service provider

The transfer must carry with it the risk of disruption to services and this will be particularly so when other major changes, such as implementing new ERP systems, are being carried out within the transition period.

In order to reduce the chance of this happening both parties must carry out their own risk assessment studies, although this could take the form of a joint pre-contract risk assessment. However, when the risk assessment is carried out it should result in an implementation plan that identifies all the really important events along the way. This plan should clearly illustrate the nature and quantity of the resources that will be required and highlight, for all to see and understand, the phased transfer of functions or processes. Overall the plan will need to allow, as far as possible, for unexpected business demands. Any element of the transfer that looks 'tight' should be analyzed in detail and every opportunity pursued to ease the timing.

> when the risk assessment is carried out it should result in an implementation plan that identifies all the really important events along the way

The senior management of both parties will need to be particularly observant and supportive in organizational matters during the transition period.

• •

The client's concerns

In addition to highlighting the areas of risk, the client's management can be forgiven for being concerned about other factors where the dangers may be more long term.

What will be the effect on the retained staff?

Typically, the provider recommends that something like the top 10 per cent of the senior staff should stay with the client, although this will vary according to a variety of factors including the number of people transferring. Experience suggests that the more senior the retained manager, the higher the satisfaction level is likely to be. Therefore the IT Director or the Finance Director will probably be happier with the new service than the other retained staff dealing directly with the outsourced team. This is natural because in all probability a higher service level will have been built into the system than existed previously, which in turn ought to create time for increased business development activity amongst the most senior staff retained.

The management lower down and closer to the outsourced service should, in theory, obtain similar advantages. Instead of spending the majority of their time in the management of people, they ought to have the opportunity, once the transfer has been completed, to spend most of their time on business development, which in turn should enhance their own career development.

Sometimes the retained middle management start to see or imagine greater career development opportunities on the other side of the fence, and some have been known to leap over it during the course of the contract. It would be surprising if the retained middle management did not start to have future career doubts during the early stages of an outsourcing. For this reason some enlightened providers have agreed to secondments for any or all of the retained management within appropriate parts of its organization and others have provided regular 'free' training courses for the retained staff.

Can a service provider's people have the same knowledge and commitment as the client's employees?

In the short term, of course, ex-employees will staff the service so the problem should not exist. However, it must be realized that even junior staff will have acquired their in-depth knowledge through day-to-day contact over months or years with colleagues in other business areas, such as sales and purchasing, or from direct customer contact. In these circumstances anything that reduces the chance of such contact could have a detrimental influence on the way the service is carried out.

Experienced service providers will recognize the dangers in losing this day-to-day contact and this is one reason why some of them now recommend that the service should be sited as close to the existing premises as possible. In other words, they recognize the need for the outsourced staff to benefit in business terms from close contact with other sections of the client's activities.

Where the service is sited close to its original or other equally suitable location and sufficient incentive is created amongst the staff to carry out a first class service, then the provider will probably be in a position to claim that nothing will be lost by outsourcing.

Where the outsourced function is located well away from the rest of the client's business activities, it would appear that there must eventually be a loss of knowledge about the core business amongst those involved with transaction processing. Some knowledge could be lost immediately if key staff are unable to relocate and the provider's chosen site is not within commuting distance. In addition, the passage of time will thin out the number of staff who originally transferred and so, in theory at least, increases the chance that the real business knowledge level is reduced.

Several service providers dispute this last point and claim, with some justification, that despite the theoretical disadvantages of taking the transferred staff away from their original business location and often even completely replacing the staff over a short period of time, they have nevertheless supplied the client with an improved service level.

> where the outsourced function is located well away from the rest of the client's business activities, it would appear that there must eventually be a loss of knowledge about the core business amongst those involved with transaction processing

Will the retained management have access to information?

The answer is to insist that full on-line access is available to all or certain specified members of the retained staff and that they can 'drill down' to whatever level of information they deem necessary.

Will the client lose the know-how necessary to carry out the work?

The client only loses those skills that it actually transfers but the retained managers will continue to have access to the skills of its former employees via the outsourcing and they ought to be fully aware of what is taking place even though they are not carrying out the activities.

Nevertheless, in the early days of IT outsourcing, many clients did find that their chance of taking the work back at the end of the first contract, or even passing it to a different provider, was severely limited because the retained skill base had been eroded. In the circumstances they could not be sure that sufficient numbers of the original staff transferring would be willing either to transfer back or to transfer to another provider. This is a difficult issue and I suspect that in some cases the management of client organizations has dealt with it by concluding that 'the contract is for five years and we may not be here after that'. If the outsourcing option is chosen then the retained management must constantly review the possibility of the retained skill base falling to an unacceptable level and take whatever steps are deemed necessary to counteract the problem.

On the subject of 'lost know-how', it often happens that when systems undergo major change valuable knowledge is lost with the passing of the old systems, even when the work is supervised by in-house staff, simply because that information did not feature in current regular reports. This is even more likely to happen when the systems are subject to re-engineering and the provider's consultants supervise the work.

The service provider's pre-contract risks and concerns

Service providers must also consider the risks involved. Rightly or wrongly they all believe that they take on most of the risk once the functions under consideration become their responsibility. But they are all very much aware that their risk can start very soon after the very first contact with the potential client because they are obliged to put considerable effort into various presentations to the client for which they are unlikely to be paid. They do this preliminary work in the full knowledge that the client is not certain to outsource, and even if it does, the work may go to another provider.

The commercial risks involved in acting as an outsourcing service provider are many and various. The actual risks and their relative degree of importance will vary enormously for each outsourcing arrangement, depending on factors such as the size and complexity of the work involved, the price quoted and how 'tight' the contract is. For these reasons, an organization contemplating acting as an outsourcing service provider for the first time should ideally have extensive experience in contracting to provide specialist services.

However, when the provider first begins a dialogue with a potential client, it is the pre-contract risks that are uppermost in the thoughts of the executives concerned.

As previously stated, the service provider starts to take on risk as soon as a dialogue starts with the client. The provider's pre-contract risks and concerns can be summarized as follows:

● being caught up in a lengthy pre-contract period during which time the provider will need to put in a great deal of effort for which it does not get paid; and

● the client chooses a provider and pursues the outsourcing option but cannot find the will or the effort required to make the change.

chapter 10

what does all this mean?

The competitiveness problem – conclusions

In the first chapter of this book I expressed the generally accepted view that the most serious problem facing management today is the absolute need to achieve and maintain competitiveness in everything the organization does. Although few people would now doubt the importance of maintaining competitiveness, I fully appreciate that this claim will appear slightly odd to many people because a manager's performance is not normally compared against relevant functions in competing organizations. In time, benchmarking techniques may develop to the extent where it is possible to make such comparisons, but they certainly don't exist today. Instead, most organizations still rate individual managers by the tried and tested method of setting an annual budgeted target and then measuring actual performance against that target. The main exception to the 'match the budgeted target' rule occurs when major projects are set up and individuals can then be set specific tasks both in terms of time and budget. However, even then there is normally no way of knowing if the targets set are truly competitive.

> achieving competitiveness requires re-engineering each service in some way to secure an ideal mix of key benefits

The lack of measurable targets inevitably means that the importance of maintaining competitiveness is largely ignored. Given this situation, it becomes vitally important to constantly remind managers what is involved if they are to strive to be competitive.

Achieving competitiveness requires re-engineering each service in some way to secure an ideal mix of key benefits. These benefits include ensuring that continuous improvement to the service takes place, making sure the image created is one of quality, maximizing speed of performance and finally, cost reduction. In other words, it is necessary to perform each group of processes as efficiently as possible given the constraints of the marketplace and available resources. Simply to aim for cost reduction is unlikely to achieve the desired goals.

The importance of being competitive is not new, but advances in technology and the resultant globalization of business make the problem far more acute than it once was. To some extent, the problem and the effectiveness of current solutions are all confused by the rapidly accelerating rate of change. The confusion was there before the creation of the internet in the mid 1990s but will become increasingly marked as time goes by.

We therefore have a situation where competitiveness is becoming increasingly important but we usually have no clear idea of how we are performing when compared to other competing organizations. In such circumstances how can any functional head really be judged on a competitive performance basis?

Lack of competitive knowledge is a prime reason for involving external specialists in the business. A leading external specialist is much more likely to be aware of competitive developments than any individual client organization.

* *

The in-house solutions to competitiveness – conclusions

When faced with yet another call on scarce resources to bring one or more functions up to the desired level of efficiency, senior management ought to be very firm in their dealings with the project sponsors. To start with, the business plan must take account of the anticipated life span of the systems to be implemented. If it is decided that it will be a minimum of five years before a further performance improvement could begin, then the minimum aim must be that the service is still competitive in five years' time. If it is fair to counter that statement by asking 'How can we possibly know how competitive it will be in five years' time?' it must be equally fair to ask 'Why spend so much money if you can not be reasonably certain of long-term competitiveness?'.

I believe that internal performance improvement projects that do not result in lasting post implementation competitiveness for the functions concerned, are not only failures, they are a waste of time, money and opportunity.

Most organizations require their managers to produce business plans for major performance improvement projects and these business plans require a trade-off. Therefore, the anticipated cost of new equipment, software, communications, consultants, contractors, etc. are added together and balanced in some financial way with future reduced costs and improved service. Not surprisingly, the vast majority of such business plans forecast future savings and improvements after implementation that at least covers the anticipated costs. My argument is that the savings and improvements need to be substantial to justify the expenditure of a major project and to be effective, they must include some promise of continuous improvement.

When projects have taken two years or more to implement, it is often difficult to measure the finished results because time has taken its toll. Customers may have requested changes to the service, and acquisitions or sales of business divisions may have taken place. Two years is a long time in the current commercial environment and a number of project sponsors have begun projects in recent times quite convinced that any failure will be disguised by changes that will inevitably be required during the project's life. Some changes occurring during the project may help to improve the chance of success, but normally the opposite is the case. Given these problems, any project team that gets close to its targets after a long project is due some measure of praise.

Getting close to or achieving the targets set may not be the same as putting the function in a lasting competitive situation. Benchmarking current and medium term competitiveness is not going to be easy or particularly accurate, but a serious attempt to achieve such a measure must surely be made before every sizeable project. If taking this action achieves nothing else, it will help to emphasize that it is ultimate competitive success that is the real aim; not achieving stage targets set by the business plan which may not be meaningful in the long term.

The fact that a performance improvement project lasts many months or years automatically means that in most organizations a further attempt is unlikely to be made within the same function for a further five to seven years. Where a project fails, therefore, this cost of lost opportunity, although almost impossible to quantify, can be substantial and in terms of future profitability, the effect may be far greater than the total initial expenditure on the failed project.

There must be serious doubts about the chances of success when trying to bring about performance improvements on a purely in-house basis. My concern is based upon the following.

> there must be serious doubts about the chances of success when trying to bring about performance improvements on a purely in-house basis

- To bring about a significant change, a major project will be necessary. However, even minor projects are disruptive, time consuming and costly.

- Even with major ERP projects covering most of an organization's functions, it is often deemed necessary to complete the work on one function before starting on another. If the whole process takes several years to complete, there is always the chance that the first function worked on will be out of date by the time the overall project is completed.

- Although it is not possible to provide accurate figures regarding the success/failure rate of internal performance improvement projects, the general perception is that a significant number fail to meet all the targets set for them.

- Even where a performance improvement project meets the targets set, there is a good chance that cost savings will be considered of disproportionately greater importance than service improvements. Unless great care is taken, undue emphasis placed on cost savings could result in redundancies that seriously limit future opportunities to recruit top quality staff.

● Even where internal performance improvement projects are considered successes, how long will that success last? If the function that has just achieved a true competitive rating is not permanently staffed by specialists and cannot recruit sufficient specialists because it cannot grow by taking on new clients – how long will it remain competitive?

As stated earlier, it is always going to be difficult to estimate the degree of success or failure for any single project if true lasting competitiveness is the target. Amongst the difficulties involved are confused or inadequate targets and the natural desire to be associated with success. For commerce as a whole, therefore, it is probably never going to be possible to give accurate estimates, because however good the research skills, the individual organizations will be loath to admit failure and will consequently disguise it.

However, I don't think it matters that we cannot be sure of the exact failure rate. We are all sufficiently aware of the major failures to accept that they do happen frequently and common sense dictates that there must be many other failures that don't get publicity because they don't directly affect the public. Add to that the admitted narrow failures and the significant number of instances where the target was not set high enough, then the situation is bound to be more dismal than is generally accepted.

I believe that if the true level of failure were known, then Chief Executive Officers would be far less inclined to approve the considerable costs involved with internal projects. Just consider what is involved in most organizations. First function A starts its project and when it is finished it is function B's turn and so on. In this way it is hoped to improve the competitiveness of the organization by applying the scarce resources needed in a balanced manner. But concentrating on one single function or group of functions at a time does not mirror what is happening in the real world, where developments tend to take place on a continuous and seamless basis across all functions.

This may appear to be a plea to confine internal projects to multi-function, totally integrated, ERP-type systems that involve almost all areas of an organization. I do accept that there is sound logic in integrating systems throughout an organization, but I am certainly not in favour of lengthy projects. Therefore, I accept that mammoth, organization-wide projects lasting many years and operating on a continuous basis are not desirable.

> internal solutions that do not benefit from utilising external specialists on a continuous basis will rarely make sense in the future

If, however, attention could be given to all the information systems requirements of an organization in a project lasting a few months instead of a few years, then an ERP type implementation could really begin to make sense. For that reason, the ASP concept of rapid Web-enabled implementations would be extremely valuable if they can be made to work for the many rather than the few. In addition, the tenure of office of senior managers is getting shorter all the time and this creates a tendency for these senior managers to ignore the medium and long term in favour of the short term. Therefore, the ASP concept is likely to match the personal targets of these senior managers whilst providing a measure of external specialist support on a long-term basis. Internal solutions that do not benefit from utilizing external specialists on a continuous basis will rarely make sense in the future.

The ASP route, therefore, offers some prospects for success with internal projects, but the skill shortage is very likely to limit use of even seemingly 'magical' new developments for some time to come, so pinning all hope in one area of technology is never a very good idea.

The outsourcing solutions – conclusions

For certain key non-core functions such as IT and finance there are, in theory, considerable competitive advantages to be obtained from their transfer to external specialists. However, many organizations have found, to their considerable cost, that outsourcing is fraught with difficulties.

Experienced observers of outsourcing arrangements will have little trouble accepting the following as factual.

1. It is possible to work with just one provider on a sole sourcing deal and yet obtain a contract that provides for an improved service at a reduced cost to the client. However, there is also a good chance that the arrangement will fail to meet the client's needs.

2. The process of working with a number of providers in the early pre-contract stages by creating a competition, will probably give the client a better understanding of the options available and so increase the chance of further improving both service and savings. Nevertheless, there is still a good chance of failure.

3. With a conventional contract the provider is not motivated to make further improvements and savings above those stipulated in the contract. If continuous improvements are made the benefits will be weighted in the provider's favour.

4. The process of motivating the service provider by agreeing to some form of partnership arrangement has much to recommend it from the viewpoint of both parties. The additional rewards obtained by the provider will depend on its ability to improve the service further than the minimum stipulated in the

contract – therefore it is not necessarily an additional cost to the client. It has to be accepted though, that even this type of arrangement sometimes fails to provide satisfaction for the client.

5 Failure of outsourcing partnership deals are most likely to occur because the service providers are either incapable of meeting the standards required, or more likely because they take on too much work and so water down their effectiveness. This raises doubts as to whether any deal between client and outsourcing service provider can ever be considered a true partnership.

6 If the basic reason why partnership outsourcing arrangements fail is because the provider spends too much time with other clients who are all looking for their share of scarce resources, then it follows that the problem would not exist if the provider had no other clients.

Separate joint venture companies set up by client and service provider would appear to get around the problem of resources being spread too thinly. There are many such joint ventures operating in this way. Typically, they are formed on the basis of the client having some special position in the marketplace and the provider creating software solutions to exploit that position. On this basis, the client's IT department and other related areas will probably be transferred to the new company, together with other services such as marketing. The service provider may also transfer marketing skills alongside software specialists, etc. Therefore most of these joint ventures depend on getting the marketing right equally as much as on the quality of the new systems development. Almost all these arrangements build in the possibility of the new company acting as an outsourcing service provider for other clients in due course. But clearly, the marketing element of this type of joint venture is always going to make comparison with conventional outsourcing arrangements very difficult.

Conventional outsourcing is subject to a range of problems, most of which boil down to the question of getting the desired share of the skills available. The outsourcing service provider might be a Mecca for the very best technical skills, but if your organization is just the latest of hundreds or thousands of clients, how can you ensure the very best service? Creating a value added, risk/reward sharing partnership will help in this respect but how effective will this be if the last half dozen or so deals entered into by the service provider were done on a risk/reward sharing basis?

● Taking advantage of the service provider's own shared service centre may be beneficial to some if the client is using the same systems as the provider. For others it may be beneficial to involve the provider in some way in the client's own shared service centre.

- For most client organizations, however, the best solution to the problem of getting the required share of skills and attention would be to own some of the service provider's equity. For the client to obtain the desired benefits, the specialist service provider must be motivated to make continuous improvements to the service during the life of the contract. Recent experience has demonstrated that by far and away the best way for the client to achieve this is to take some measure of equity in the provider to ensure that it is always going to be a favoured customer.

for most client organizations, however, the best solution to the problem of getting the required share of skills and attention would be to own some of the service provider's equity

Some other conclusions

1. Services such as catering, cleaning and security are widely outsourced even though they exist without constant pressure to implement new technology. These services tend to get outsourced because they are seen as separate businesses and they are easy to outsource because they are rarely entwined with other areas of the organization through technology in the way that IT and Finance are. With all other functions, however, the pressure to outsource is largely based on the desire to achieve a measure of competitiveness by utilizing the latest information systems. The fundamental competitiveness problem is, therefore, usually related to changes in technology even where HR, Finance, Call Centres and other functions are being outsourced. I accept that many of these BPO areas are outsourced without the management concerned even considering the information systems factor. However, even these managers will accept that it is the constant change brought about by the development of technology that is fuelling the organization-wide pressure to become competitive by outsourcing.

2. Quite clearly, the future technology needs of the organization is the most important area to deal with. There is a good argument for saying that until you are happy that the core IT function has reached a competitive standing and is likely to remain there, then other functions should not be subject to performance improvement projects.

3 Although outsourcing arrangements are fraught with problems, the use of external specialists offers the potential for improved service, cost reductions and continuous improvements that cannot normally be achieved by in-house teams that do not have the benefit of continuous external help and guidance. This factor will remain the main reason for outsourcing.

4 Projects covering a single function or group of functions that proceed on a 'fire-fighting' basis are not normally suited to most organization's real needs.

5 If a business function does not have the capacity to grow, it will not be able to attract the best and most skilled employees.

6 For an internal function to achieve continuous improvements it will normally need to be:

- core
- capable of continuous growth
- in a position to attract the best employees
- in a position to take on new clients.

7 For a service provider to perform well for an outsourcing client the following must apply:

- the provider must be an established specialist;
- the provider must be capable of recruiting top quality staff;
- the provider must be motivated;
- the client must be a very important customer.

The overall conclusion must be that it is essential for all organizations to strive for lasting competitiveness. To achieve this goal, continuous involvement by external specialists is necessary, however, getting these specialists to concentrate fully on your service is easier said than done.

chapter 11

an alternative way of approaching
the competitiveness problem

The most important conclusion from the last chapter is that to achieve competitiveness the client organization needs to involve an external specialist. However, to maximize the chances of success the client needs to take some equity in its chosen provider to ensure that it always receives first call on the skills available.

> to maximize the chances of success the client needs to take some equity in its chosen provider to ensure that it always receives first call on the skills available

I fully appreciate that it is going to be very difficult for even major client organizations to obtain such an equity stake in existing outsourcing service providers. The alternative, as I see it, is for client organizations to create and build their own service providers.

In this chapter I am going to suggest ways in which organizations of various types and size might go about creating their own providers. However, for many, these notions might require a leap of faith that is difficult to contemplate. In other words, some readers might react by concluding that it might work for others, but it would not be suitable for them at the moment. For that reason I have prefaced my ideas with the following story, which indicates how one group of normally very staid organizations have benefited from taking radical leaps of faith into the outsourcing world.

In an Executive Report on outsourcing finance for The Institute of Chartered Accountants (ICAEW) publishing company in 1995, I included the paragraphs shown below.

> If we imagine an industrial estate of ten small manufacturing companies on the edge of a provincial city we would all accept that each company would need some form of security. In turn most of us would agree that it would not make financial sense for each company to set up its own security system from scratch, each with spare sets of security guards, dogs, etc. for emergencies.
>
> What is so very different about the finance departments? Even if each of the ten manufacturing companies has different systems, staff levels and degrees of integration into other parts of their business, what's to stop some entrepreneurial accountant or accounting firm taking over responsibility for all the accounting functions on the industrial estate and developing a system to cover all of their needs?

The above extract came from a section of the book in which I was trying to establish the following five points.

1   Although the outsourcing of finance was then largely limited to major organizations, i.e. major clients and major providers, the situation was likely to change as the concept took hold.

2   Outsourcing is best carried out on a local basis.

3   It would be difficult for a firm of auditors to provide adequate outsourcing services in finance if they were not also IT specialists. This was likely to remain true whatever size the firm was and whatever size of client they were dealing with.

4   It would require qualified consultants and specialists to bring about the necessary changes and continuous improvements. Not all auditing firms are so endowed.

5   Despite the above 'qualifications', new opportunities were opening up for entrepreneurial firms of accountants.

After the report was published, a number of people contacted me regarding this idea and in turn I extended my reasoning in a couple of articles. About a year later I was asked to address the annual meeting of the ICAEW's general practitioners group. The general practitioners account for virtually all the ICAEW members working as auditors outside the big international firms. Obviously, my task was to explain what was happening in financial outsourcing and to explore with them any potential new markets.

I expected that most of the delegates would have little interest in the ideas I was presenting and in that respect I was not disappointed. Nevertheless, many others were sufficiently interested to move quickly into a non auditing environment and over the following days and weeks many of them kept me informed of their plans. These were typically to target potential clients in their locality that were not already auditing clients.

The most important discovery made at this conference, however, was that a number of firms were well ahead of me. One firm had effectively given up auditing altogether and concentrated instead on providing comprehensive business process services over what was a relatively small geographical area. They had in fact started by targeting local business estates. Others were using the internet to promote their services. Very soon, articles appeared in the national newspapers explaining how British firms of chartered accountants were doing the daily accounts for both local and international companies. One firm was even receiving the daily accounts by fax from a manufacturer in the former Soviet Union.

> one firm was even receiving the daily accounts by fax from a manufacturer in the former Soviet Union

I anticipate that more and more firms of chartered accountants will obtain business in this way. Nevertheless, without extensive discussion and publicity, my view is that growth in this business area is going to be relatively slow. Let's face it – it is difficult to bring about a change as fundamental as this in long established organizations. Apart from challenging the very concept of shareholder accounts and even the need for professional qualifications, it might also suggest to some accountants that auditing is being exchanged for low-grade work. After all, there are non qualified or poorly qualified people making a living by acting as part-time accountants for one or more small manufacturers and service companies in most towns.

Other reasons, such as an aversion to selling, may limit chartered accountancy firms from developing this business area quickly, unless the internet comes to their rescue or their potential clients were to see these firms as outsourcing service providers independently. But if some firms of chartered accountants can make the enormous leap of faith by becoming outsourcing service providers, then it should be possible to think of other ways of meeting the competitiveness challenge.

I have suggested above that outsourcing arrangements are more likely to work for the client organization that obtains a large measure of control and ownership of the service provider than one with less control and ownership. But how would a client organization set about obtaining equity in one or more service providers?

Business satellites

At this point I would like to introduce the concept of 'business satellites'. I believe that the concept could be applied to organizations of almost any size and any description.

The business satellite concept will not be necessary for an organization that:

- can honestly claim that its non-core functions are competitive now and will remain so in the future;

- despite past changes which might have involved the releasing of middle management, they can justifiably claim that there is sufficient growth potential in its non-core functions to attract the best qualified staff;

- can guarantee that the next technology project will be implemented in a competitive timeframe, at a competitive cost, will meet the targets set for it and will provide a competitive advantage for many years ahead;

- will shortly re-engineer its non-core functions in such a way that a long-term competitive advantage is assured;

- will meet development needs by ensuring that the highest quality of staff is always available for such work;

- can ensure that where outside specialist help is required, this will be of the highest possible quality, will be cost effective, will avoid or limit internal disruption and will produce results that guarantee a competitive advantage for many years to come;

- will use the best service provider available for any outsourcing arrangements which will result in providers making substantial service improvements, costs savings, continuous improvements in a situation where the organization is a key client and each month the provider strives to do even better than in the previous month.

I suggest that any organization that cannot be positive about the issues detailed above could benefit by setting up a business satellite (BS) programme. Before I describe a BS programme in detail, I want to explain my thinking a bit more.

1 I am not saying that organizations should dispense with management techniques such as business process re-engineering. I believe these techniques have played and will continue to play, a valuable part in modern business. I am, however, saying that you should both understand their limitations and your own success rate at handling past projects of this type.

2 I am not saying that organizations should ignore the potential for improvement offered by the implementation of ERP systems and other technology developments that might integrate the business processes. Far from it, the logic of developing integrated systems has been apparent for a very long time. The trouble is that ERP systems are probably still at a development stage comparable to that of the motor car in the 1920s, with the mechanics and drivers belonging to an even earlier era. I accept that as they exist, they cannot be ignored, and that most sizeable organizations have to bite the bullet and buy them. It is, however, essential not to consider them the ultimate solution to the competitiveness problem. Management does not solve its competitiveness problem just because an ERP implementation has been completed.

> management does not solve its competitiveness problem just because an ERP implementation has been completed

3 I am not arguing against the use of management consultants. Without doubt the dramatic benefits, in terms of performance improvement, achieved by some major organizations probably would not have been possible without help and advice from these specialists.

4 I am not making the BS suggestions as a means of holding back the tide of change. I accept that more and more people will work for themselves in various types of contracting roles in the future, but I don't necessarily think that this heralds catastrophic short-term changes in the way organizations are managed. I accept the concept of the virtual organization – but I doubt that many of the organizations already in existence today will have achieved virtual status by 2020.

In summary, no human being can see what the future will bring, but we have to make decisions that constitute our best estimates. Forecasts of the future may be useful in concentrating the corporate mind on the competitiveness problem, but without positive action they cannot be a solution to the problem. All the usual solutions start from the assumption, which is normally correct, that the situation is desperate and that this, of necessity, requires a major firefighting exercise. Very few people could justifiably claim that their internal projects and outsourcing arrangements are the result of a carefully thought out long-term plan.

> forecasts of the future may be useful in concentrating the corporate mind on the competitiveness problem, but without positive action they cannot be a solution to the problem

Is there a way of dealing with the competitiveness problem that allows for long-term planning and an easier alternative path to salvation? The BS programme looks for this easier path.

A BS programme is based on the following principles.

1 Most organizations will want to perform core functions in house but will be willing to consider the advantages of passing non-core functions to specialists in those business areas.

2 In-house performance improvement projects for non-core functions tend to fall short of meeting the targets set for them.

3 However beneficial outsourcing might be in theory, it is not easy to be sure that the service provider will remain committed to ensuring the best possible service for each and every client.

4 The greatest chance of outsourcing success is likely to arise in situations where both client and service provider have a financial interest in making the arrangement work. This must go far beyond simply meeting the contracting details in order to obtain a specified fee. In most cases some form of joint venture will be necessary.

5 The technology factor is the key element in maximizing the performance of non-core functions.

6 The development of BS programmes should not result in too much extra pressure, financial or mental, being placed on management. In any commercial environment the best way to avoid pressure is to plan ahead. With BS planning ahead is straightforward, because having accepted that it is the technology element that is causing the problem, management is free to create one or more parallel IT organizations to duplicate and later take over the functions controlled by its current information systems. The time from creation of the BS to its takeover and control of existing systems can be flexible. A BS could therefore be set up for a function that is currently being subjected to a performance improvement project or is already outsourced.

7 Being empowered to do your own thing and working for an organization in which you have a financial stake is an ideal incentive for producing excellent work.

The following theoretical example illustrates how BS programmes might work.

How a local authority might develop a BS venture

Smalltown District Council (SDC) is a relatively small council close to the borders of a large provincial city. The chief executive of SDC believes that the problems they face are getting worse month by month. A project starts with the express aim of establishing which processes should continue in house and which would be done better if they were transferred to external specialists. Eventually, the project management committee reports that in a number of areas of work where information systems are involved, the externalization option should be seriously considered. Other areas not involving IT are recognized as potential candidates for outsourcing but there is general agreement that all these activities should continue in house until the IT requirements are fully understood and accounted for.

Following this conclusion SDC decides to begin a BS programme. It is informed that the first step in the programme is to set out all its key business processes and, if possible, separate them under their controlling functions. The object is to find those processes that are failing or likely to fail completely within, say, a three-year period and to see if it is possible to find a partner or partners for these services.

When the areas using IT were rated in terms of 'the most urgent to deal with', the most important area turned out to be Housing Benefit. This was surprising in some ways, in that this service had actually been outsourced four years previously and was the authority's only experience of outsourcing. Furthermore, the arrangement was proceeding according to plan and was showing SDC reasonable savings when compared to the last in-house costs.

The problem currently faced by SDC in this area is that they now think that they are being seriously overcharged. Normally speaking, a function as relatively small as housing benefit would not be outsourced in isolation from other similar business processes. SDC took the step to outsource almost in desperation. A few years previously the council had been subjected to a number of unforeseen problems, including an unexpected influx of people from outside its own boundaries. The result of this was that claimants were waiting excessive periods of time to make claims and would often return several days after making the original claim, only to find that their details had not yet been entered into the system.

> normally speaking, a function as relatively small as housing benefit would not be outsourced in isolation from other similar business processes

After studying the situation in 1996, SDC was convinced that it should immediately outsource this function. However, the operation was relatively small and only one service provider expressed serious interest. When this provider finally took over responsibility it quickly involved document image processing (DIP) specialists. The result is a system in which the claimant is directed to a small desk in the authority's main reception area where the relevant benefit claim details are immediately scanned into a computer. Then, by the time the claimant has reached the main housing benefit desk, the details are up on the screen and the claim can be processed.

The contract has one year to run and the service provider has already informed SDC that it would be willing to sign a further five-year contract at the existing price plus 1 per cent annual increase to compensate for inflation.

On the face of it this appears to be a genuine offer made by a fair minded service provider, particularly as the first contract was priced at roughly 75 per cent of the authority's own costs. SDC's management does not share this view. For one thing, claims are currently at least 25 per cent fewer than four years ago, but, more importantly, it has become apparent to a great many people that due to the use of DIP and other technology, the provider is using only 40 per cent of the staffing that SDC used. Consequently there is now a widespread view that the provider must be making a substantial and unacceptable profit from the arrangement.

SDC's management feels uncomfortable and threatened by this situation. In recent times they have tentatively approached other service providers, but now doubt that any of them will come up with a substantially better deal than their existing provider is offering them.

Much of the internal criticism stems from the view that the service could now be done in house at a considerable saving on current outsourcing costs. Several internal mid-ranking managers have put forward the view that the DIP technology is no longer that special. They also argue that the provider appears to be staffing the system without any obvious technical back up. Nevertheless, senior management recognize that taking the service back in house will involve considerable risk for an organization that is short of the required technical expertise in most areas of activity. This is the basis on which the housing benefit function was included in the study.

When senior management study the project team's findings they see a potential answer to their problem. There are several other business processes, both existing and potential, that could benefit from either the type of treatment the original provider gave to housing benefits, or from being associated with the housing benefit work. There is a temptation to offer this extra work to the existing provider but they decide against it. Instead, the management accept one of the cornerstones of BS – that to be sure that you have the best chance of becoming and remaining competitive the client must have a financial stake in the provider.

The overall logic of the SDC scheme is as follows. The internal IT department has never really performed at an acceptable level and there are real doubts that the authority will ever be able to attract people of sufficient quality to change this situation. Nevertheless, their own experience of outsourcing, their size and the problems that have been related to them by other authorities all point to the conclusion that they should shy away from any conventional outsourcing agreement. Consequently, they resolve to maintain the status quo as far as the IT department is concerned but to let it be known that they will shortly create a fledgling IT development company which they hope will one day take over all their own IT work and that of other organizations in the locality. They stress the local aspect of the concept by arguing that environmental needs will in future limit home to work commuting.

They hope to ensure the continued strength of the existing IT team by telling its members that they will have the opportunity to work alongside the new company on any work that is obtained privately and in due course, providing targets are met, there will be an option to transfer to the new company. A further 'carrot' is created by the statement that individual equity in the new company will be open to existing IT department members for exceptional performance.

To make sure that the new venture will have every chance of success, SDC's management believes that just one area of IT activity should be targeted in the first few years. Not surprisingly, they decide to concentrate on housing benefit work and the other related areas.

However, the level of current authority work in the areas under consideration is relatively low and they have no short-term way of knowing the potential for the satellite company to sell its services across the local business community. Without being able to quantify the short-term potential of the new venture, they prudently decide on a three-year development period before the satellite company takes full control of the targeted areas. Accordingly, they negotiate in advance with the current supplier of housing benefit services a new two-year deal for existing services only. This gives them a breathing space of almost three years to grow their own service provider.

In accordance with government guidelines, they contact all the other local authorities in the area and put the idea in some detail to each of them. Although some of these authorities initially show enthusiasm, it turns out, after six months of talks, that none of them has quite the same agenda as SDC.

Identifying joint venture partners

The next step is to begin a search in the local area for a small organization that would make a suitable joint venture (JV) partner. Initially their search was confined to small existing local IT companies, but after a number of initial discussions the SDC management decided to widen the target to include other small organizations with a growing IT development capability. Eventually they found one organization that looked suitable and where all the principals were excited about the potential outlined by SDC.

> the next step is to begin a search in the local area for a small organization that would make a suitable joint venture (JV) partner

This is a three-partner firm of chartered accountants. One of the trainee accountants at this firm has developed his IT skills to a high level. The firm has benefited not only from his improvements to their own financial systems, but has gained considerable goodwill and fee income from contracting him and his small team out to clients. One area in which he has been particularly innovative has been in creating small but sophisticated networks. The trainee and his firm have had to pay a price for his success. His studies have suffered because he has spent an unusual amount of time on IT work. The shortage of study time problem is likely to get worse because he has recently married and his wife is now expecting a child. Just prior to SDC approaching his firm, the young man had informed the partners that as he was unlikely ever to qualify and become a partner, he was giving them as much notice as possible that he would soon look for a new position or start his own business. He indicated that he was ambitious and now believed that he had a future as a developer of IT systems. In return for being open about this he hoped that he might be considered for contract work in the future. As a growing number of competent and successful IT specialists are now working under the direction of the trainee accountant, the partners have much to lose.

Joint venture arrangements

Within a few months of finding this joint venture partner SDC had created a new small limited liability company with a start-up capital of £100,000. The ownership is split 80 per cent SDC and 20 per cent to the chartered accountancy firm. However, half of SDC's holding (40 per cent of the total) will be transferred to certain key people who meet agreed targets within a two year timeframe.

Amongst these key people will be a marketing and sales manager recruited to begin the initial sales foray into the local marketplace, the IT specialist from the accounting firm and any other new employees who make a substantial contribution to profitable growth. The shares will be allocated in a way that both takes into account the perceived difficulty of the task set and their performance against target. Any shares not earned by performance will be retained by SDC. A maximum of 25 per cent of the total share value of the company will go to the new ventures people if they meet the targets set for them. In addition, SDC will use the other 15 per cent as a carrot for relevant authority employees who have demonstrated that they have added value to both the joint venture and the authority during the initial two years.

Benefits and drawbacks for SDC

The management at SDC will always have first refusal on the expertise and services to be developed by the new company. They believe that this will provide a very useful technology 'back up' in a number of business areas. In particular they believe that by the end of the second outsourcing contract for housing benefit services, the new company will be able to provide a replacement service at a much reduced cost to the authority. Other benefits include the following.

1. Management will be seen as taking prudent steps to stop excess profits going out on a continuous basis to the current outsourcing service provider.

2. It will be demonstrated that it is possible to work for a local authority and yet still benefit from the equity opportunities found in the market economy.

3. The IT specialist and possibly others will still work for their original organizations for part of each month in the early stages. Consequently the new venture will not have to fund all their costs.

4 With luck, the authority may have created a profit return that can in future be used to offset local taxes.

5 The authority will have created a pilot scheme that can be repeated and improved upon for other business process areas.

Drawbacks will include the capital at risk, which will always need to be kept to the minimum, the time taken to get the project underway and the risk of failure.

> drawbacks will include the capital at risk, which will always need to be kept to the minimum, the time taken to get the project underway and the risk of failure

Benefits and drawbacks for the chartered accountancy partnership

For this firm the benefits are as follows.

1 They get a reasonable stake in a new technology venture for a relatively small outlay.

2 They dramatically improve their chances of keeping the services of their IT specialist on a part-time basis in the short to medium term.

3 They would gain experience of an outsourcing/shared services environment.

4 They might hope to build up a good working relationship with SDC which could in turn lead to other business opportunities.

The drawbacks will include the very small risk of losing their £20,000 of capital.

Benefits and drawbacks for the IT specialist and other employees of the new venture

Here the benefits would appear to include the following.

> **1** The opening up of new career opportunities without risking their current jobs or losing the advantages provided by their current jobs.
>
> **2** The opportunity to get an equity stake in a potentially strong local company operating in a high technology environment without risking their own capital.

The drawbacks are difficult to identify. If the venture fails they will be in no worse a position and they will have gained valuable experience.

SDC's second joint venture

Shortly after setting up the company described above, SDC came across a second potential joint venture partner. This second organization is based in a high street shopping area and promotes itself as a specialist graphic designer. Despite this claim, much of the current workload involves selling stationery and printing letterheads. However, the owner has considerable graphic design skills and has obtained a reasonable reputation as a designer of websites. More importantly, though, he can demonstrate real potential as a publisher, both on and off line. In addition he employs two young women as graphic designers and both show considerable potential in publishing. At the time SDC approached this company both women worked on a very part-time basis as they had children of pre-school age.

Unfortunately, the overall flow of work for the business has increased only marginally over the last few years, due to a major decline in the retailing business. Firefighting work in this area by the owner has often resulted in dramatic periods of boom and slump. The owner was rapidly coming to the conclusion that the retailing element of his business was in terminal decline, but it was actually taking up an increasing amount of his own time as he had been forced to make other retail staff redundant. However, he had serious doubts about his cash flow situation if he suddenly stopped retailing. Consequently the amount of effort he could put behind obtaining new design work declined rapidly and he began to question that he would ever be in a position to offer full-time work to both the other graphic designers, even if they wanted it. Of more short-term importance to him was the knowledge that the women also had doubts about the future of the business and had been involved in preliminary discussions about starting their own business if sales did not improve. In the circumstances the owner was willing to listen to SDC.

The parties decide to set up a new company that will concentrate solely on internet developments. The start-up capital, ownership and allowance for future share distribution mirror the situation for the first JV.

Benefits for SDC

SDC sees the following benefits in this second arrangement.

1   It has created an inexpensive unit to exploit the future potential of the internet in general and publishing in particular.

2   It has some internal work that can profitably be transferred to the new venture.

3   It is aware that many of its own IT and other staff are contemplating internet projects.

4   It has created a second venture that SDC's existing specialists can move in and out of as the work dictates.

5   It has a second company that will attract good local talent and which it hopes will grow to become an outsourcing service provider of one or more of SDC's functions.

6   It has a second company that may be in a prime position to eventually offer other local companies an outsourcing service on an ASP basis.

Benefits and drawbacks for the owner of the graphic design company

The owner of the graphic design company sees the benefits to himself as follows.

1   He will considerably increase his long-term chance of success in an area he wishes to concentrate on.

2   Although he has to find an additional £20,000 for his part of the venture, this is balanced by the security of obtaining other short-term work from SDC. As a result he will be able to rationalize his original business with fewer cash flow worries.

3 He will hope to balance the highs and lows of his current operation by being able to move his existing staff between the two organizations as business dictates.

4 He will be able to keep the two graphic designers in his original business on a part-time basis.

5 He will hope to sell more goods and services to SDC.

For him the only drawback is the risk of losing the capital invested in the new company.

Benefits and drawbacks for the employees of the new venture

The benefits would appear to include the following.

1 The opening up of new career opportunities without risking their current jobs or losing the advantages provided by their current jobs.

2 The opportunity to get an equity stake in a potentially strong local company operating in a high technology environment without risking their own capital.

Again, the drawbacks are difficult to find. If the venture fails, the employees will be in no worse a position and will have gained valuable experience.

• •

Further explanation of the business satellite examples

I appreciate that providing an example in which a local authority is the prime mover in creating new joint venture companies may appear a little odd. Obviously, one would naturally expect the commercial world to initially show the most interest in a new business idea. However, I believe that any organization from either the public or the private sector which employs 50 or more people might benefit from creating a BS programme.

I used the SDC examples because I wanted to demonstrate that the concept was also open to the public sector and because I believe that local authorities now have the freedom to take all the actions I've described. I believe that few local authorities would now have problems with the first JV because the aim is clearly to overcome an existing problem. On the other hand, I am aware of local authority executives who would find the underlying profit motive behind the second JV totally unacceptable. But why should this be a problem in the twenty-first century? Governments in various parts of Europe are taking gradual steps to allow public sector departments to embrace commerce, so why not take the opportunities on offer?

> I believe that any organization from either the public or the private sector which employs 50 or more people might benefit from creating a BS programme

When I have raised this issue with local authority doubters, the reasons that come back include not having either the time or the right type of employee, and not wanting to damage local businesses by competing with them. The first two of these arguments might be valid in the short term, but if they remain valid for the medium and long term then management is seriously at fault. The problem of competing with local businesses cannot be a genuine factor in the current commercial environment. Small businesses of almost every description are under increasing pressure from a growing number of competitors of local, national and international origin. Therefore, those businesses that collapse from local authority competition would have collapsed from other commercial activity if the authority had not been involved. Surely every local authority must do its utmost in the future to reduce the burden of local taxation.

The term 'radical' can be used in two ways. It can be used to describe an advanced and probably controversial view, which by its very nature would be applicable to only a small number of organizations in the short term. It can also be used to describe sudden dramatic changes. I believe that the BS concept cannot be described as radical in either of these senses because it aims for a planned anticipation of information technology growth over a reasonable period of time. Conversely, an organization forced into a major internal project or outsourcing arrangement because it had failed to do the necessary forward planning should accept that it is being forced into a radical step. In other words, it is being forced into a dramatic change and there is a good chance that failure will result.

Some people may question the advisability of employees working for more than one master, and although this practice is increasing, I am aware that failures as well as successes can ensue. Nevertheless, because equity will be available for a job well done, it would be up to the participants to ensure success.

I would like to explain further the reason for stressing the importance of the local aspect in the example given. I accept that modern communication developments have made the world a much smaller and convenient place to move around in. I can also see that software products intended for use in Europe might be put together just as well and, currently, far less expensively in, say, India, than in Europe. But for the most part the major internal projects and outsourcing arrangements deal not with the basic software but with the application of the software, and this is a local issue that is best dealt with by on-the-spot advice. You might be able to arrange for the design of a vehicle by sending your ideas and requirements to a company on the other side of the world, but once the product was manufactured, the designer would not then be in an ideal position to advise on a particular problem with your car.

Outsourcing service providers will normally argue that they can handle a client's application equally well at a base many thousands of miles from the client's main site as they could next door to it. Furthermore, they will probably be able to produce customers who will support their claim. However, I have noticed that when a client insists that a separate service is set up for it away from the provider's other activities, then the provider will often stress the benefits of being next door to the client. These benefits arise from being close to the hub of the client's business with the resultant opportunity to fully understand the underlying strengths and weaknesses in areas like marketing, manufacturing and distribution. In addition, it is true to say that commuting problems in the Western world are both a continuing nightmare for those that have to do the commuting and a serious threat to the environment. The BS concept, if widely practised, would help to reduce this problem.

Finally, I would like to raise a subject that I have not covered in the earlier chapters but which is nevertheless fundamental to the BS concept. This relates to the marked difference in the number of IT professionals who may be available for work and those willing to take a conventional job.

We are constantly being reminded from books, films, television programmes, etc. that over the last few thousand years great civilizations have been spawned in various parts of the world. Invariably, they have flourished for a time and then died. In these successful cultures of ancient times, an environment was created either by accident or design, and for perhaps just a brief period of time, that allowed far more people than normal to get involved, contribute and prosper. However, the key factor for success was usually some form of slavery imposed on most of the population.

> as each new community has been offered the opportunity to embrace wage slavery it has usually been gleefully accepted

When the industrial revolution dawned in the later part of the eighteenth century, success was largely dependent on a new type of slavery – wage slavery, which was usually considered preferable to the alternatives on offer. Until very recently only a small percentage of the world's population were in a position to indulge in developments that could really improve the standard of living of their families, their locality and the world community as a whole. As each new community has been offered the opportunity to embrace wage slavery it has usually been gleefully accepted.

Historically then, the ideal environment for the development of human commercial creativity has come about only on those occasions when both a climate of opportunity has been present and sufficient individuals with the necessary skills have been encouraged in some way to take up the opportunity.

There is no doubt that thanks to the development of the PC and modern communications techniques, the opportunities for technology and business creativity are open to more and more people with every day that goes by. Equally, the number of people obtaining the necessary basic skills in order to avail themselves of the opportunities is increasing day by day. Nevertheless, the skill shortage, which is a key factor in the competitiveness problem, remains with us. It remains a problem because the people obtaining these skills increasingly do not want to conform to the conventional work pattern. In effect they are not willing to pick up the opportunity in the form it is offered. IT specialists are probably the first major group of workers who are in a position to refuse wage slavery.

People involved in IT recruitment over the years are well aware of the marked decline in the number of IT specialists who are now willing to relocate. Why should they when they can be reasonably sure of a similar job becoming vacant within their own locality in the short term? True, they might have to work as a contractor on occasions, but they will put up with this and any related travel due to the fact that, in a way, they are working for themselves and because they recognize the more contracts they do, the more experience they get. As they are constantly being made aware, every other day somebody with only comparable skills to their own will become rich simply because they were in the right place at the right time. In such circumstances few experienced IT professionals worth their salt are going to be satisfied with an ordinary 9 to 5 job in an organization that does not specialize in developing technology.

As a breed the IT specialists have always appeared different from other professionals. Now I find that the younger IT specialists, both male and female, feel and act differently in other ways. Quite often they express a collective desire to adopt green issues and codes. A great many of them don't want to commute long distances daily and they don't want to work for organizations they find ethically unsound. Equally, they are not very keen on working full time for some organization that they consider boring when they can earn sufficient money for their needs on part-time work or taking on a contract once in a while. Many people will feel that this is an irresponsible attitude, but why take a permanent job when by taking the part-time contract route you can earn as much money for fewer hours worked and yet end up with a much more impressive CV?

I believe that the BS concept offers an ideal carrot and challenge for most IT specialists, both young and old. During the industrial revolution the opportunity was there for a large number of creative people to make themselves rich and to create work and further opportunities for others. These opportunities were taken up at an amazing rate for the time, but it was noticeable that the most creative companies produced the most new entrepreneurs. It is equally noticeable that the companies currently at the cutting edge of technology tend to produce most of the people who go on to become technology entrepreneurs in their own right. In part this may be because they have employed high quality people, but it is also because in most cases, some form of equity has been available, as a carrot, for outstanding work.

Go on – create a BS programme and give yourself and the other would-be entrepreneurs a chance to get a firm grip on competitiveness and at the same time provide a boost to your local community.

appendix a

• •

starting the outsourcing process

Once the client has taken the decision to outsource, there are certain pitfalls that it must understand and avoid in its search for the ideal outsourcing relationship. The aim of this appendix is to highlight these pitfalls and suggest a step by step route to overcome them. It is assumed that the client organization wishes to create a competition between potential service providers for its outsourcing business.

Finding a suitable partner by creating a competition

In order to create a competition it is necessary to establish which outsourcing service providers appear to be suitable partners and then make arrangements to contact some or all of them.

The established method of dealing with a range of potential suppliers of technology and knowledge systems is to send out Invitations to Tender (ITTs), or Requests for Proposals (RFPs).

Over the last decade or so an accepted methodology has developed for structuring these requests and this is normally adhered to when sending out outsourcing RFPs. Typically, the suppliers are asked to explain how their service will deal with each of the requirements specified. In creating the RFP, care is taken to structure the way the answers will be provided. In this way the writers hope that when they get the information requested, they will be able to compare each provider's offering 'like with like' and create a 'level playing field' to facilitate future decision making.

In theory, the use of RFPs can overcome some of the initial problems faced by companies wishing to outsource. It should enable the potential outsourcer to give its own explanation, in as much detail as it thinks necessary, of its requirements and expectations from an outsourcing arrangement. This document may then be sent to a number of potential service providers, thus establishing an element of competition. The additional advantage is that the competing service providers should have all the information they need to create their bids without each sending their own fact-finding teams to repeatedly disrupt the potential client's staff.

However, the RFP is a tool that must be used wisely if it is to produce the desired effect. It frequently happens that a great deal of effort is taken up in preparing an RFP,

the RFP is a tool that must be used wisely if it is to produce the desired effect

which then fails to produce the desired response from potential service providers. Very often this is due to two main causes – too much detail was included and the service providers were not approached correctly.

Clearly, it is important to get the right amount of information in the RFP and this must be set out in a way that maximizes the possibility of an accurate response. Unfortunately, it is often mistakenly assumed that the right amount of information is, quite simply, as much as possible. It is not unusual for an outsourcing RFP to take months to prepare, when it might well have been better prepared in just a few days.

Often, an over-detailed RFP stems from the desire to ensure that service providers have absolutely all the relevant information in one document, in order to prevent them all from visiting the site to talk to the staff and take up the potential client's time. It is essential that the providers be given all relevant information. However, too often, the client's staff resorts to taking paragraphs from existing reports and documents in order to 'beef' up the document. As a consequence, RFPs sometimes contain extraneous information that confuses the potential bidders. The clients must not only remove all extraneous matter in developing the RFP, they must search for ways of getting the information over using as few words as possible whilst ensuring that the statements are not misunderstood.

It is in both parties' best interests that the correct level of information is included in the RFP. For a single function outsourcing an adequate RFP might cover no more than 30 to 60 A4 pages with the description of each process taking up no more than two pages. It is only going to be possible to get an 'indicative' bid in response, but this is the maximum anyone can expect from an initial proposal and an indicative bid should be sufficient for the client organization's purposes at this early stage.

The poor approach problem stems from the fact that these RFPs are often sent to potential service providers with very little prior warning and preparation. The combined result of too much confusing detail and too little contact is that the service providers may actually be reluctant to respond to the RFPs.

What prospective outsourcers frequently fail to take into account is the amount of time and effort necessary to produce a bid in response to their overly-detailed RFPs. Major providers will have specialist staff dedicated to dealing with RFPs but even for them, more effort will be needed for responding to a one-off outsourcing RFP than to typical software ITT. For outsourcing service providers, the RFP may require too great an investment of time on the part of senior management and valuable staff to justify making a bid unless they have a reasonable expectation of success.

The provider needs to believe, firstly, that the prospective client is reasonably likely to actually carry through its stated intention to outsource and, secondly, that it is competing on a level playing field against an acceptable number of rivals. Providers generally seem happy with their chances if they are one of three rival bidders, but become doubtful about the odds if the RFP is sent to many more than that.

A wise potential outsourcer will do well to narrow down the choice of service providers in advance by researching the suitability of those in the marketplace. It should then approach the chosen few before sending out the RFPs in order to assure them of its intention to judge the bids fairly and, except in unforeseen circumstances, to go through with the outsourcing.

Experience shows that an excessively detailed RFP, representing a great deal of work for respondents competing against a large field of known competitors, will cause many service providers to either decline to bid or to prepare a far more simplified response than the client wished for.

Clients often fail to anticipate these problems because they have relied on their experience of producing invitations to tender (ITTs) for software suppliers and the like. In theory, software vendors will always be happy to receive an ITT; they get much of their business from this source and will have staff dedicated to the task of responding speedily and accurately to ITTs. In addition, almost all

> in theory, software vendors will always be happy to receive an ITT

organizations setting up a project to assess their software requirements will, in the end, purchase new software from one source or another. A software vendor responding to an ITT that had been sent to a total of five companies would, therefore, assume that its chances of making the successful bid were a healthy 20 per cent.

It follows then that if the client has been careful enough to restrict the request to companies whose software ought to provide a 'fit', then there should be a good response. To have a 20 per cent chance of obtaining a substantial contract and having the staff available to deal with such requests would appear to provide all the justification necessary to ensure that the software vendor will always respond eagerly and carefully. However, in practice, expectant software purchasers sometimes find that some vendors do not bid at all and others complete the templates in the easiest way open to them without going into the detail requested.

If a detailed RFP is sent to five potential outsourcing service providers with little or no prior contact, then they are almost certain to respond less favourably than their counterparts in the software industry. For a new IT outsourcing, each provider will probably estimate the chance of a contract ever being signed at a maximum of 75 per cent, but for non-IT areas the estimate may be as low as 40 per cent. In these circumstances, the provider can be excused for thinking that the statistical chance of success could be as little as 8 per cent even if they start on equal terms with the competition. Given this situation any provider who gets the RFP out of the blue will naturally be reluctant to respond. Not unnaturally, they assume that the potential client must be in discussions with at least one provider and consequently they have been included to make up the numbers.

Creating an RFP and dealing with the providers

If, despite the drawbacks involved in outsourcing, an organization still feels that it is the most appropriate course of action to follow, there are steps that can be taken in order to improve the chances of a successful outcome. The method described in the following pages is intended as an example of good practice which may help to cut down on the risks whilst maximizing the service level and savings to be obtained from an outsourcing arrangement. This step-by-step procedure is a development of one first published in 1996, in *Outsourcing the Finance Function* by J. Brian Heywood, Accountancy Books Group, Institute of Chartered Accountants for England and Wales.

First step: collecting the basic information

An organization that ensures that it has all the relevant information before beginning discussions with service providers is likely to save in time and effort and gain in terms of credibility with those it wishes to deal with. When management consultants are brought in to advise on the outsourcing process, the wise client will find that there are fewer costs involved in assigning its own staff to gather the basic information rather than leaving it to the consultants to collect. The information should, therefore, be gathered before consultants get involved.

The information may be divided under a number of headings, as follows. It should be noted that only information which is strictly relevant to the initial discussions needs to be divulged to potential service providers at this stage. The RFP should not contain more information than is required for constructing a bid.

The required information

> *Staff numbers in the functions to be transferred* – in practice, only about 90 per cent of people will usually end up being transferred, with the remaining 10 per cent being the top management levels in the function, who will remain with the client. At this earliest stage in the assessment, however, it is a good idea to base assumptions on the highest number of staff who could be transferred. It is important to include all the people necessary to perform the functions concerned, including any short- and long-term contractors. From this it will be possible to gauge the number of full-time equivalents involved. It should not be necessary to pass on the information about total staff numbers until the choice of service provider has been made and a strong indicative bid received from the successful one.

Chart each process – create a breakdown of the number of staff who have an input into each area and the amount of their time thus used.

Management and location of each function – this should include a description of the management reporting structure in each area. Also, a note should be made of any important points related to the locations, such as any property held on a different basis from the majority of the organization's buildings, for example a short-term rental arrangement.

Explain the service currently being delivered – e.g. for an accounting function it might be important to outline the output by ledgers, reports, transaction type and quantity with any marked seasonal variation. It will also be important to provide the current performance levels and the real trend in performance levels. For a marketing and sales function it might be necessary to summarize the size of the market being targeted over a reasonable time period, and show how market share had changed. It would also be necessary to briefly explain marketing/sales tactics and to explain how and why they differed from the main competition.

The IT area – it is useful to include a summary of IT if it strongly influences other functions that are being outsourced. The required information will include equipment by number and type, number of PCs, main software used and networking details. It will also be necessary to explain special services provided to internal and external users, all projects, either under way or planned and give a description, including the condition, of legacy systems. If there is any pressure for major change, then it is worth noting where this pressure is coming from and what changes are suggested. If any functions or processes are already outsourced, these should be noted, along with any problems with the existing service providers that are anticipated.

> if there is any pressure for major change, then it is worth noting where this pressure is coming from and what changes are suggested

Alternatives – details of alternatives to outsourcing which have been or are being looked at.

Give background details on the company – an overview of the company origins, culture and current status, including ownership, number of employees and market share, with any anticipated changes.

What is the reason for considering outsourcing at this time? – is the reason strategic, such as a desire to outsource non-core functions in order to spend time and effort on the core business, or tactical, for example, a cost saving exercise.

Joint venture possibilities – is there any chance that software or other products could be developed for sale to third parties as they are being created for use in house?

Anticipated contract length – clients should give their expectation of the length of contract they would be willing to award, along with the anticipated timing.

The limits of service provider involvement – for the functions to be outsourced, the client should consider where it believes the line should be drawn between the responsibilities that it wishes to retain and those to be passed to the service provider, i.e. those processes in and out of scope. At this early stage in the proceedings, it will not be necessary to give potential service providers more detailed information other than which of the main processes fall on either side of the line. Quite frequently, service providers will convince the client of the desirability of including additional processes within the outsourcing scope, but that's another matter for a later time.

Second step: begin a dialogue with the providers

The first and second phases of the process, before the RFPs are sent out, are often not seen as particularly important by the potential client. However, if some thought is given to preparing the ground in advance with the service providers, the final arrangement is likely to be more satisfactory.

The first task is to decide on the providers to be approached. Ideas on finding the organizations are explained in the main body of the book.

If the client feels that it would not be in its best interests to disclose its identity in the short term, then outside facilitators will be needed to make this initial contact. However, in most cases, by dealing with the provider's senior management and stressing the need for security, the client should find that it is afforded sufficient confidentiality.

It is important to make contact with the provider's most senior people first to establish ownership. All other things being equal, a 'sales opportunity' passed down by the CEO is more likely to remain of interest than one that is passed up the management chain. It will be obvious, at this point, that the information given to the providers must be couched in terms that make them keen to compete for the contract.

Another main aim is to establish the suitability of each provider, in order to narrow down the field of competition. Those chosen should represent a good match for the client's culture, as well as having a thorough understanding of the functions to be out-sourced, the technical ability to achieve the desired improvements and a healthy urge to win and perform the work on offer.

The client must therefore realize the importance of the first contact with the provider. In a nutshell, the provider's initial aims will be to establish how likely the potential client is to eventually outsource; how valuable a client it will be and the degree of competition intended. For their part, the client's representatives must try to establish the suitability of each provider on the basis of culture match, understanding of the functions to be outsourced, ability to bring about the improvements envisaged and how hungry it is likely to be for the work on offer.

> a provider is far more likely to have confidence in a client who even during this pre-RFP period is able to answer the questions and back them up with figures

This should illustrate the importance of making advance contact with the providers in order to 'warm them up' ready to receive the RFP. The client should take pains to reassure each potential provider of the sincerity of its intentions to outsource, its value as a potential client and that the competition for the contract will be fair and open to no more alternative providers than is reasonable.

At this point, the providers will not yet have received the RFP but the client will never-theless reap the rewards of the work carried out in Step 1. Although they will have been asked to wait for the RFP, the providers will usually have many questions to put to the client before receiving the RFP. Experience would suggest that these questions should be tolerated to some extent and every effort made to develop a warm relationship. A provider is far more likely to have confidence in a client who even during this pre-RFP period is able to answer the questions and back them up with figures. For tactical and competitive reasons, however, it is normally acceptable to give transaction details but not manning levels.

The typical provider will naturally assume that the potential client who has all the information available 'at its fingertips' has put substantial thought into the outsourcing process and is, therefore, likely to see it through. A provider who gains respect for the client at an early stage is likely to proceed happily, expecting that this helpful efficiency will continue during the pre-contract and transition periods.

It is never necessary to provide detailed figures to the providers at this stage, so most clients should have few qualms about answering their questions. For example, questions on the extent of the general ledger activities are best answered with annual figures for accounts, cost centres, inter-company transfers, entries and accruals, and the number of cost/profit centres and a description of the reporting process will normally suffice when information on reporting analysis is sought.

This pre-RFP period is not always afforded much thought by the potential client, but if it handles these initial approaches well, then it will have gone a long way towards achieving a good outsourcing arrangement.

Third step: developing the RFP

It must be remembered that the competition induced by sending out RFPs is in the client's interest but not necessarily in that of the provider. If the only difference between two prospective clients is that one is offering a sole sourcing arrangement and the other is seeking to pick a provider by means of competitive bids, any provider will choose the former.

Competing for outsourcing work is a costly business, in terms of both time and money. If a potential client is large enough, most providers will still choose to bid even if they do not rate their chances particularly highly. Over time, though, it is likely that the costs involved in bidding will drive providers to reconsider these tactics even when major potential clients are involved. It may be, for example, that competing is only cost effective if the success rate is at least one in three. In that eventuality, it may be decided that competing for any contract with more than one other provider will not make sense, as even if they win as often as the competitors do, on one in three occasions the outsourcing may not go ahead at all.

The ideal number of providers to whom the RFP should be sent is never likely to be more than three or four. By engaging in discussions with a range of available providers in the initial stages, it should prove possible to limit the field to a few suitable ones who are likely to respond to the RFP in the way the client wishes them to.

The RFP should contain a mixture of general and specific information so that the providers can make a bid without recourse to additional sources of information. Bearing in mind the danger of too much information being presented and the fact that an experienced service provider will in theory be able to make a reasonable indicative bid from the transaction details alone, the following has been known to suffice.

Introduction to the company

the RFP should begin with a brief description of the client organization, including its history, recent trading situation and current ownership

The RFP should begin with a brief description of the client organization, including its history, recent trading situation and current ownership. If there is any likelihood of acquisitions or sale of business units with any bearing on the functions to be outsourced, then that should be explained in this section. In addition, details should be given of the process to be followed before approval can be granted for outsourcing. One or two A4 pages should probably suffice for this information.

Background leading up to the RFP

This should include a description of the functions to be outsourced, with any additional relevant information such as the age and effectiveness of the systems in use. It will also be worth explaining the triggers that lead to consideration being given to outsourcing in the first instance. From these, the client's expectations of an outsourcing arrangement may be better understood.

Details should be given of any projects, current and planned, relating to the functions to be outsourced or which may have an indirect effect on these functions.

Confidentiality

In some cases, clients ask potential providers to sign confidentiality statements before they receive the RFP. Others may include a confidentiality form with the RFP, with a request that it is completed and returned as soon as possible.

The basic processes

In order to ensure that time is not wasted while providers gather further information from the client, each process must be described accurately and in some detail, but not in so much detail that the provider is held up by the need to plough through unnecessary description. For basic processes, there is unlikely to be a need for more than one to three pages of explanation.

Objective or purpose – the main reason for the existence of the process or function, e.g. in describing an accounting process it might be to obtain monies due or provide information on trade debtors. In a marketing function the objective or purpose might be to achieve targeted sales.

Included in the scope – a list of the processes to be outsourced.

Outside the scope – a list of the processes to be retained in house.

Transaction details – normally these need only be shown on a per annum basis, therefore in the finance area it might be sufficient to state the number of live customer accounts, number of invoices, number of credit notes, etc. For a marketing and sales function it is normally sufficient to detail the number of annual sales emanating from the various sales channels. However, if the function is subject to marked seasonality, such as 40 per cent of sales or invoices happening in the immediate pre-Christmas period, then this will have to be adequately explained.

Strengths and weaknesses of existing systems – this section should describe the feeder systems, any manual input, file maintenance and the various outputs. It is important that the weaknesses should be explained truthfully in detail.

Current working practices – if there is any additional information that will help to describe how the current service operates, it should be given here.

> *New system requirements* – the client's hopes and expectations of the effects of the outsourcing arrangement on services, including a time scale for achieving the desired improvements.

Timing requirements

It will be necessary to determine a timetable for the completion of projects to be carried out in the transitional period. This should be fully described in the RFP, ensuring that there is no room for misunderstanding these timings, especially in the case of critical projects.

IT strategy

The outsourcing of a function such as finance or distribution may require new systems to be created by the service provider. Such systems are unlikely to be entirely stand-alone and may require the creation of new interfaces with the systems operating in other functions. The overall IT strategy of the client organization is therefore of great interest to the potential service provider even when a function other than IT is being outsourced.

> the overall IT strategy of the client organization is therefore of great interest to the potential service provider even when a function other than IT is being outsourced

One to two pages will probably be required for a detailed description of the client's overall IT strategy. There should also be some idea given of the progress made towards completion of any current projects, for example, where the client organization is in the process of moving to an ERP solution. If there are any factors in the current IT strategy and policies which may have the effect of setting limits on the actions the provider might wish to carry out in respect of other functions, then these should be explained in detail. A description should also be given of the prevailing standards, to which the provider will be expected to adhere.

Critical success factors

It is worth bringing the critical success factors together under one separate heading, although they will probably be detailed elsewhere in the relevant parts of the RFP.

Transfer of staff

It is vitally important that the transfer of staff is handled properly and according to the relevant regulations. Each party must agree from the start on what share of the responsibility it will be taking. The client should set down its expectations as to when its responsibilities will end, preferably also giving details of its normal redundancy package.

Ideally it should set a date, which may or may not be the end of the transition period, after which the provider will take responsibility for redundancies.

Transitional arrangements

A separate heading in the RFP will be required if the client wishes to specify any essential conditions regarding the apportionment of costs during the transitional period.

The RFP should also include the following items.

1   The required contract period – for a first contract this should not normally exceed five years. If a provider wishes to base its bid on a different time period, then it will need to fully justify this deviation from the RFP.

2   A requirement that staffing levels and costs should be quoted in terms of the basic processes as well as for the overall service.

3   A requirement that costs should be provided for each year.

4   A request that the bids should include the amount of input, in working days, that will be required from those staff retained by the client, during the transitional period. This factor may significantly affect the cost-effectiveness of the different bids.

5   A request that the transition costs, broken down into the periods to which they apply, should be shown separately.

6   A request that any system development costs should be detailed in a similar manner.

7   A request for background information on the service providers themselves. The client will wish to consider how the culture, people, locations and relevant experience of the providers fit them to work with its own organization.

8   A request for details of the providers' experience of TUPE or other relevant regulations and transferring staff.

9   A request that the providers' methods of operating fixed price and partnership type contracts should be explained, together with their preferences for either of these.

10   A request for details of the providers' personnel policy with regard to their own staff and for a statement as to whether transferred staff would be covered by the policy.

Other points

If the client will require the service provider to perform any major additional tasks, such as the creation of new systems, these should be described in the RFP in sufficient detail to allow the providers to be able to produce an indicative bid.

Different situations will require different ways of dealing with the question of when or if the providers should take over property or equipment and, at this stage, it may not be necessary to raise the issue.

The providers should be asked how they would deal with unforeseen but nevertheless common problems such as the mid-contract sale of either service provider or client and future acquisitions and divestitures by the client. Often both parties enter an agreement without this issue ever having been aired. Sometimes it is discussed but both parties agree to meet such problems if and when they happen. Experience would suggest that leaving this subject to chance is a mistake when an appropriate clause in the contract will at the minimum provide a framework in which to renegotiate the relevant parts of the arrangement.

> the RFP should make it very clear that the decision to outsource will depend on the price quoted and the risks being satisfied

The RFP could contain a template, to assist the service providers in composing a response to the RFP that meets the client's expectations. Otherwise, the desired format and contents of the response should be explained clearly.

The RFP should make it very clear that the decision to outsource will depend on the price quoted and the risks being satisfied.

Fourth step: help the providers with their bid

The RFP will give a closing date for the submission of responses. However, whilst the bids are being prepared, the client would be best advised to maintain contact with the providers.

It may be that information has been missed out of the RFP, or that certain clauses have been worded badly. A client who talks to the providers as they are evaluating the RFP will be able to spot such problems and clear up any potential misunderstandings before the bids are finally delivered. In addition, it is always worth ensuring that the relationship with the successful service provider is given the best possible start. Contact and assistance at this stage in the proceedings can help to ensure that the eventual agreement begins in an atmosphere of mutual respect and goodwill. The client must, of course, be scrupulously careful to ensure that no help or additional information is given to one provider without also providing the same information to all the others.

This is also a good time to assess the question of culture and chemistry compatibility. Even though contact between client and service provider staff may have been limited, it is still worth beginning an internal dialogue to establish how comfortable the relevant client managers are with the competing providers. If this information is documented at this point it will be of great help later during the short list negotiations stage, to determine which, if any, of the positive and negative views are really justified. Obviously an outsourcing arrangement is going to work much better if the individuals in both organizations are comfortable with each other and their aims are compatible. Some service providers are so sensitive about this that they make a point of telling all potential clients, at least twice during the first contact, how fortunate it is that the two organizations have a perfect culture match.

Fifth step: evaluating the bids

Ideally, all the providers will have responded to the RFP, having been helped by the efforts of the client to make the process a straightforward one. However, in practice, some bids will be lacking in certain detail. If this is the case, it should be possible to request additional information to fill in the gaps and ensure that the responses can be judged on all the relevant criteria. It is unlikely that any provider will refuse to supply such information, having put in the necessary effort to reach this stage of the proceedings.

Sixth step: getting close to a decision

In some cases, even at this stage, when it has competitive bids from two, three or more potential service providers on the table, the client is still considering whether to outsource at all. Assuming that the bids suggest that there is something to be gained from doing so, most clients will proceed at least a little further. Where there is any suggestion that a service provider will be able to offer an improved service at a reduction to the current cost, then the client must have a sound justification if it chooses not to follow up this option.

Although it is difficult to argue against the logic of creating a competition, there are dangers if the competing providers are not handled correctly during the bidding process. To start with, it will be natural for the bidders to assume that price is likely to be the key factor. They will know from past experience that it is often the only consideration, whatever the client has previously indicated.

Therefore, if long-term competitive advantage is the real aim it will be necessary to ensure:

● that the people evaluating the bids are not overly influenced by the price factor. The important consideration should be 'How will each of these bids affect our competitive situation in each of the years covered by the contract?'

● that the quality of the service, long-term competitive advantage and desire to create a successful relationship between the parties are stressed as the key elements at all times when negotiating with the bidders. There are good tactical reasons for playing down the importance of price at this relatively advanced state in the negotiations.

> if the emphasis has been too strongly placed on the money issue, the effect on the winning provider may be quite negative

The importance of these two points should not be overlooked. All too often, the short-listed bidders are left with a final impression that cost is everything. In the circumstances there is a tendency for the providers to cut the projected fee a little more because they have already spent a great deal of time on the project. Quite naturally this will affect the quality of service they intend providing. If the emphasis has been too strongly placed on the money issue, the effect on the winning provider may be quite negative. The lasting impression will probably be that they only won the deal because they bid too low, so they will immediately set out to correct the situation. It is worth noting that the person managing the project for the successful provider will be judged first and foremost on the profit produced.

appendix b

●●●●●●●●●●●●●●●●●●●●●●●●

before contemplating the outsourcing transition

● ● ● ● ● ● ● ● ● ● ● ● ● ● ● ● ●

The need to plan

Before the transition gets underway it will be essential for each step of the transfer to have been planned in detail and every effort made to ensure that the staff, both those retained and those to be transferred, know what is expected of them. The contract will have been finalized and signed and any necessary pre-contract consultancy and other fact-finding work completed.

The transition relates to the period of time necessary to complete all the changes required before the transferred function or functions are finally placed under the direction of the service provider or joint venture management. Prior to the transition, the client's staff will have carried out the entire workload, but by the end of the transition the ongoing work will be carried out by the new team. In a conventional outsourcing arrangement the transferred staff make up around 80 per cent of the new team with some long-term additions or changes of personnel made by the provider.

In some outsourcing arrangements though, the transition is completed in distinct phases, which effectively result in responsibility being transferred before all the planned changes are completed. This can occur when a project area within the scope of the relevant functions is not considered a major contributor to service improvements or substantial short-term savings and both parties agree that work on it can be safely postponed. However, it is most likely to happen when part of the overall project is dependent on some other work being completed, which is outside the provider's control. Both parties should agree on a risk management plan in advance of the transition if there is a real risk that progress might depend on the successful completion of projects outside the provider's control.

When a provider believes that there are major factors that it cannot completely control, it will naturally become concerned that problems of someone else's making could occur before or during the transition. Service providers faced with such a situation usually request that the client accepts responsibility for all the costs up to the end of the transition. Clients forced to accept this request frequently end up paying the provider a management fee to cover its own costs up to the end of the transition. Clearly, when these circumstances prevail, the contract will normally only come into being once the transition has been completed. In most other circumstances the contract is effective from the start of the transition. Pre-transition work is normally covered by an agreement for consultancy services.

Outsourcing an important function is a major step for any organization, particularly if it is contemplating such an arrangement for the first time. In truth few organizations begin discussions with service providers believing that outsourcing is the only likely option or outcome. The service providers are well aware of this and fully realize that even though they may have responded to an RFP and made follow up presentations, outsourcing may still be one of several options being considered by the potential client.

From the point where outsourcing becomes a serious option the client will be constantly trying to balance the benefits and risks involved.

The very fact that outsourcing is such an important step to take, makes a strong case for suggesting that the decision should not be made in haste. With that in mind it is often a good idea to create a 'breathing space' before the service provider is given the 'go-ahead'. If advisers are involved, their opinions should certainly be sought but the final decision ought to be made at least a week after they were last seen to allow key internal staff time to develop their own independent views.

> once outsourcing becomes the preferred option and at least one provider has been isolated, then the preparation to outsource should begin very quickly

However, once outsourcing becomes the preferred option and at least one provider has been isolated, then the preparation to outsource should begin very quickly. Independently from its chosen service provider, the client should begin to map out certain key areas in detail. In these key areas it will be necessary to evaluate and re-evaluate the requirements and timing on a regular basis before the contract is signed.

If the client makes little or no preparation prior to finalizing the decision to outsource with the chosen service provider, then it will always be playing 'catch-up' with an organization that starts off being much more knowledgeable about the subject. This appendix, therefore, concentrates on the pre-planning work that should ideally be done before a successful provider is chosen and at the same time goes into more detail about some of the more technical aspects of outsourcing that are only briefly covered in the first part of the book.

It has been suggested to me on more than one occasion that it ought not to be necessary to do pre-planning work of this type. 'Surely if we are going to put so much trust in this service provider why can't we just let them get on with it and tell us what they want from us?' This is best answered by considering the treatment of transferred staff – an area where it is obvious that client and service provider will both be united in their desire to treat the staff fairly. It will certainly be in the provider's interest that the client plays its part in keeping the transferred staff up to date with developments, but the provider may not have advised a client on this subject before and in any case it has its own problems. Although it is in the best interests of both parties that the employees are treated with respect it is still an area that the client must pay careful attention to. As stated earlier, a client who alienates the transferred staff by its failure to plan ahead and keep all concerned fully informed, is taking unnecessary risks with the quality of the future service.

It follows that the importance of pre-planning will be much more important for the client in areas where the aims of both parties do not exactly match.

Some of these areas are considered below:

- service level agreements

- service performance measures

- continuous improvement programmes

- management of the contract.

Service level agreements

Service level agreements (SLAs) are the link between the specifications laid down in the contract and the delivery of the service. In essence they provide the basis of the legal framework under which the performance of the provider is measured.

SLAs naturally vary according to the requirements of the various parties to the outsourcing arrangement. But in each case the quality of the service delivery will depend to a large extent on these factors.

- How well both parties have isolated and set down the really critical controls. Although agreement will be necessary, it will be apparent that the client must set its own agenda and not just leave it to the provider;

- In an appropriate risk/reward sharing arrangement, creating a dynamic, but flexible service that accepts that changes to the SLA are inevitable and a fact of life if maximum improvements are to be achieved. The ideal SLA for this purpose should concentrate on the service required rather than detailing the methods of obtaining it.

- Creating and laying down easily understood service control and service performance metrics. The wise client will attempt to look for continuous performance improvements and where possible build them into the service performance metrics.

- Setting up the required quality management and performance review processes.

For each activity it will be necessary to agree both a standard of service and the critical performance indicators. It is

> for each activity it will be necessary to agree both a standard of service and the critical performance indicators

important that the various processes are grouped into distinct service activities so that they can be dealt with separately and the performance measures can be directly applied to them.

Each activity will need to be clearly defined. This will require a description of its purpose, the volumes involved and the service expectations. In effect the full process is described in sufficient detail to avoid the chance of confusion and misunderstandings. Similarly the service required should be given the same amount of attention to detail. The performance measures are normally tasks and deadlines. In due course they will be compared against the contract standard requirements on accuracy and timing.

It sometimes happens that client organizations reach the pre-transition stage having only recently carried out an exercise that has resulted in full descriptions of the activities to be transferred. Unless this exercise was done previously with outsourcing in mind, it will still make sense to draft out the desired service again and analyze the likely consequences, before starting in-depth discussions with the provider. Not surprisingly the minimum service tends to go up a few notches when outsourcing service providers are likely to be involved.

The actual service level agreements produced will depend on the nature of the processes being outsourced, but typically they will cover the following areas.

operational requirements – minimum communication needs, timescales, back up system requirements, security, etc.

support levels – the minimum technical support necessary plus any improvements required, when they will take place and maintenance.

changes in volume and type – how changes in volume and type of work are to be dealt with.

the personnel – the structure of management, key responsibilities and quality levels of the important management roles. The number, skills, experience, etc. of other key staff should also be detailed.

minimum service levels – this area is frequently limited to bare statistics, e.g. the service will be available 98 per cent of the time. Again, the wise client will give this considerable thought. The real aim should be to stipulate the minimum level without trying to tie the service provider down to an unreasonable level.

a procedure for resolving disputes – it is very important that the procedure for dealing with disputes is laid down in terms that cannot be misunderstood.

Service performance measures

Each group of users should be required to detail their service reporting needs. Ideally these users should start by documenting how this service has traditionally been achieved followed by the changes they now wish to see and the reasons for them. If advisers are involved they should be requested to independently document any changes or improvements they would recommend. Although this will involve a small amount of additional time and effort when compared to the combined project approach, it does allow senior management the opportunity to double check that errors are not made due to 'too many cooks' being involved. Although the service provider will eventually have a strong input to these measures, it makes good sense for the client to initially set out its own requirements so that there is a clearly documented statement of ideal service performance. Theoretically, it must be against the client's interest if the service provider is allowed too great an input into these measures early in the proceedings. Nevertheless, it sometimes happens that the provider will independently suggest measures that favour the client more strongly than those originally suggested by the client.

The individual activities in the SLA are normally all given their own targets. With risk/reward sharing arrangements these targets are often set, initially at least, on the basis of a modest improvement on what the client's own staff have been achieving. Many such arrangements allow a reasonable period of time for the provider to make improvements after which penalties will apply if the target is not met and a sharing of savings takes place if they are significantly bettered. Clearly, these targets cannot finally be set without the agreement of the service provider. Despite this, it makes sense for the client to seriously consider targets, penalties and rewards before beginning the final planning stages with the provider. This is another area where it is advisable to seek help from the provider's current clients.

Quality assessments are necessary on a regular basis comparing the SLA and actual performance. Independent quality assessments might also form part of the agreement. In this scenario third-party consultants are employed at agreed intervals to do benchmarking studies. These studies are then used when necessary to adjust baseline service levels. Quality assessment exercises are useful in identifying those areas where the risk of failure is most acute, but they will often also illustrate areas where continuous improvement projects might be justified. Usually, quality assessment work does not begin until the provider gets involved.

It goes without saying that all quality assessment and performance targets must be capable of being measured. These measurables can be 'scored' in terms of quality, quantity, time elapsed, satisfaction or any other measure jointly agreed as important by both parties. Achieving clearly understood measurables is not always a simple task.

> all quality assessment and performance targets must be capable of being measured

In fact, it is sometimes very difficult to measure factors like quality and accuracy. Nevertheless, the metrics built into the SLA must be as devoid of alternative interpretation as possible. To achieve this aim it is essential that these metrics are put together by both parties. If there is still any chance of misunderstanding, appropriate 'notes' or 'schedules' should be made to the SLA. These changes will be legally binding under the contract and will have to be agreed by both parties, but they can occur at any stage in the life of the contract.

Ultimately, both parties will need to agree on a timetable to take the service from the pre-transition stage to the baseline service stage – usually the first day after completing the transition. If the client has done little or no work in defining and scoping the service until the transition starts, then it will have to work considerably harder over the following months than it might otherwise have done. More importantly, it is very likely that all this work will need to be under the direction of the provider in order that a reasonable timeframe can be achieved.

Continuous improvement to the service

Sometimes the transition begins with the provider leading a joint project team seemingly intent on making one single leap towards complete competitiveness. ERP projects intended for completion by the end of the transition often come into this category. Common sense would normally indicate that something as major as an ERP project would be better left until the two parties had gained experience of working together. Against that, I have observed several outsourcing arrangements where the alternatives to a completely new integrated software system to begin the contract appeared even less attractive.

In most outsourcing arrangements, however, one of the key aims of the transition and any pre-transition projects deemed necessary will be to identify both the service improvements that can be achieved in the short term and those that are better left to some future date. Typically the short-term changes will concentrate on improvements in reliability, speed and quality of the existing service while at the same time searching for cost reduction and rationalization opportunities.

Risk/reward sharing or value added outsourcing arrangements will normally require the provider to look for opportunities to re-engineer and improve the service at regular intervals both during the transition and thereafter as new processes, interfaces, reports and greater on-line access to information becomes possible. Logically, though, the heavy workload experienced and the process of both parties learning to work together means that improvements first isolated during the transition are usually implemented much later.

Many of the highly publicized added value success stories in outsourcing have come about because of continuous improvement programmes created sometime after the contract got under way, i.e. the actual improvements were not anticipated prior to or during the transition. The existence of this knowledge has led some client organizations to feel that if they create the right risk/reward-sharing environment for the providers to work in then it is not an area that needs exercise their minds in the short term – certainly not prior to the transition starting.

Unfortunately, there are certain aspects relating to continuous improvements in the future that the client organization has to consider very seriously and as early as possible in the pre-contract period. This is because continuous improvements are unlikely to all start and end conveniently within the confines or boundaries of the function being outsourced.

It is possible to imagine all manner of out of scope problems that the provider might face when contemplating future improvements. Related areas may have already been outsourced to one or more different providers and these other providers or other internal departments may be proceeding along entirely different agendas with new projects planned or under way. Obviously, a new provider is unlikely to take on a function without previously establishing who has control of the related functions. However, potential confusion in the out of scope areas may not be sufficient to stop the provider going ahead with the basic contract. In other words, just having the contract with only the possibility of sharing future savings may be sufficient reason for the provider to sign up for the arrangement.

In these circumstances the provider may have entered the agreement with every intention of seeking continuous improvements providing that the client gets its house in order at an early stage after the contract starts. If the provider is prevented from bringing about further improvements due to factors in other related functions that it is unable to influence, then it can be excused for assuming that the problem lies with the client. After all, it does not have an unlimited supply of the specialists who bring about such improvements. Consequently, it only requires a few setbacks when attempting to bring about improvements to convince the provider's management that the specialists could be better used elsewhere. It is possible that this change, in terms of reducing future creative effort, could come about without the client ever realizing it.

Therefore, if it is seeking continuous improvements from an outsourcing arrangement, the client must analyze the potential for inter-department or inter-supplier co-operation and discuss its findings with the provider before the transition gets underway. Convincing the provider at an early stage that it understands these potential limitations and will do everything it can to correct the situation should help to create the right sort of environment for continuous improvements.

Management of the contract

Over the last few years a certain degree of standardization has developed in the way that the outsourcing contract is managed. Most often this involves a management team of over the last few years a certain degree of standardization has developed in the way that the outsourcing contract is managed

equal numbers of client and provider executives on a joint review board or steering committee which meets on a regular basis during the life of the contract.

The steering committee will probably come into being at the start of the transition. It will be apparent that normally the transition will comprise a whole range of special and probably 'one-off' projects to bring about the required changes. At the end of the transition new projects will be less frequent and take up a smaller amount of the available resources as the service beds down and something approaching normality returns.

On occasions one person has successfully managed the transition and then gone on to do a perfectly adequate job for the duration of the contract. However, most people would argue that these are very different roles requiring people with different backgrounds and mental outlooks. The person managing the transition will actually be managing a number of separate projects such as:

- location change – which may involve creating a new infrastructure, purchasing and installing new equipment and relocating staff;

- counselling and transfer of staff including preliminary training;

- selection, installing and implementation of new systems; and

- the transfer, setting up and management of the ongoing service.

Typically, the project manager for new systems will have been supplied by the provider and the project manager for the existing service by the client.

The person managing the transition is often termed the Programme Manager. This person must be an experienced project manager used to managing a range of technology and other projects of major size and cost. The position will probably disappear after the transition is completed and this is one reason why the role is usually given to one of the provider's most senior consultants. Logically, if the service provider takes leadership of the transition it will wish to make the Programme Management appointment from one of its own people.

Once the transition has been completed, new management must be found to manage the ongoing contract. Typically, the provider will appoint its own contract manager and this may or may not be the person responsible for the service delivery. The client's own contract manager can come from anywhere, in theory, but usually the job goes to one of the project managers involved in the transition.

Client organizations should give early and serious thought regarding the person they choose to manage the existing service project during the transition. It is not unknown for the client to make this appointment from an executive it intended to retain after the transition only to find that the circumstances have evolved in such a way as to make his or her transfer inevitable.

The success of the ongoing outsourcing arrangement will depend to a large extent on the ability of the managers involved on both sides. It is, therefore, of vital importance at an early stage in the pre-transition negotiations to consider the range of skills, experience and personal qualities that are necessary to perform well in this position. The ideal ongoing contract manager will have:

- experience of the functions concerned;

- the ability to feed the right level of information up and down the management tree;

- sufficient technical knowledge and common sense to anticipate problems;

- the ability to build relationships with the individuals involved;

- a genuine belief that the service can be continually improved.

The steering committee will probably meet quite frequently during the transition, often once a month at first but probably less frequently thereafter. Overall the steering committee will be responsible for:

- ensuring that the existing service is sufficient to meet the client's needs;

- a continual analysis and review of the performances of both client and provider in order to stop potential problems from developing;

- approving the appointment or dismissal of key staff involved in providing the service;

- approving any changes necessary from the contract arrangements; and

- the overall performance of the management.

Other factors worth considering prior to the transition

- Experience shows that some transitions have been spoiled by unexpected problems related to the use of new facilities. Typically, this happens most frequently when new facilities are required close to the client's existing facilities. In such circumstances it is natural for the client's management to accept responsibility for finding these additional premises. However, management who are not experienced with the problems of finding and furnishing premises have often underestimated the time taken to complete such tasks. It would be unrealistic to try to allow for all eventualities and it will be clearly beneficial to both parties to complete the transition as quickly as possible. Nevertheless, both organizations would be wise to use the period just before the transition to make doubly sure that the timing agreed upon for all key issues is actually achievable.

> experience shows that some transitions have been spoiled by unexpected problems related to the use of new facilities

- Many clients see advantages if the end of the transition coincides with the accounting year end. Most service providers will try to abide by this wish if at all possible. However, the transition period already contains many risks for both parties, so care should be taken to understand all the ramifications of this or other 'nice to have' additions to the overall project.

- During the first few weeks of the transition both the retained staff and those being transferred will be working at a much more intense level than in the past, as they get to grips with problems relating to both the ongoing service and the new developments. Extra pressure and the need to bring about change usually increases tension between staff members during conventional internal projects. In an outsourcing arrangement, the added complication of one group of employees transferring to another employer is almost bound to add to the tension. In the circumstances both parties will do well to prepare all concerned for the problems that are likely to occur along the way and any client that assumes that it can safely leave these problems to the provider under the terms of the contract is asking for trouble. If the transition is not completed successfully a good proportion of the problems resulting will remain with the client's retained staff.

The service provider finally assumes control

Typically, a month or six weeks after the service provider assumes control a certain 'calm' descends upon most members of the retained management and the transferred staff. However, difficult or easy the transition may have been, the majority of the client's former employees could be excused for thinking that the situation is 'returning to normal'. Given the circumstances they can be forgiven for being optimistic that job security, in particular, will be the norm from now on. Why not be optimistic? The ongoing service will be carried out by people who were there before outsourcing was ever considered, and with fewer staff and specialists on hand the service must be efficient now and should remain so in the foreseeable future!

For those people that have transferred to the service provider there is the additional possibility that they have joined an organization that will achieve above average growth in the coming decades. Consequently the transferees from a non-core function will, on average, obtain greater rewards, job satisfaction and security than those who have not been outsourced. However, most of these rewards will only be available if they are able to achieve continuous improvement for the clients they work for. They are employed purely to provide a service and because that service represents their new employer's core business it must be continually improved. The attitude adopted by the most up-to-date and creative providers is that they have to keep their clients' service competitive and that can only be done by continuous improvements to the way they produce these services. Transferred employees are required to find new ways of making improvements and savings which in turn, in theory at least, puts pressure on their own chances of long-term employment. Any fears in this direction are, however, counteracted by the potential for taking on other clients' work and the prospects for transferees to become specialists in their own right.

Those employees who have been transferred in a risk/reward partnership arrangement will need to understand quickly what they are committed to. From the start of the ongoing period to the end of the contract, and probably beyond it, the service must be continually refined, updated and improved by:

- continuous improvement programmes

- customer service improvement measures

- quality control programmes

- service performance reports and evaluation

- continued staff counselling, training and development.

Towards the end of a typical transition, both parties usually become convinced they have too little time available to do justice to the relative importance of the projects being developed. The provider may be able to bring in additional key specialists on a temporary basis but the client is rarely in a position to make up lost ground so easily. The moral of the story is that the client usually needs to plan for the transition earlier and more efficiently than the provider just to arrive at the winning post at the same time.

Finally, it is worth stating that the wise client manages and massages the contract until it comes to an end. It is of vital importance that every opportunity is taken to assist the provider to improve the service, but it is equally important that steps are taken to keep the provider 'on its toes'. To achieve both these ends the following are worth considering:

> the wise client manages and massages the contract until it comes to an end

- involving end users in monitoring service delivery against targets;

- working continuously on improving the relationship with all the provider's staff;

- building in the right to review the relationship and contract at various stages along the way;

- making sure that you maintain the right to invite tenders for new consultancy and outsourcing work.

appendix c

● ●

the essential elements of
the contract

It is in the nature of outsourcing arrangements that no two are exactly alike. In this Appendix we look at the range and type of issues that both parties to such an arrangement will need to address but it is not intended for use as the basis of a draft contract. The unique nature of each outsourcing arrangement should be incorporated into its own legal documentation.

Another point to be aware of when drawing up an outsourcing contract is that there will usually be factors that cannot be quantified or measured until much of the transition work has been completed. Hence, many outsourcing arrangements begin with a qualified contract. For example, the initial phase of the work may involve studies into issues such as the SLAs, the baseline charges and the method of calculating the risk/reward elements, the results of which will have a direct bearing on how the latter phases proceed. In ideal circumstances, these studies should be carried out prior to negotiating the contract, but if this is not possible, then the contract must contain the assumption that agreement on these issues will be able to be reached.

In spite of this assumption, it is essential that such a contract makes provisions for the possibility that agreement will not be reached. In this eventuality the contract will need to be terminated at the end of the transition or soon after and there will need to be an agreed mechanism for the division of the costs incurred.

1 The contract structure

The agreement will normally contain the following information.

> **1** The names and addresses of both parties, the dates on which the contract will start and finish and a precise description of those areas of the client's organization to which the outsourcing agreement relates.
>
> **2** Guidelines and, where applicable, rules for the management of the transferred service, along with a description of the responsibilities of each of the key managers. In addition, management disagreements between the parties should be anticipated and a framework should be set down for dealing with such situations.

3 A detailed description, with full technical explanations, of all services affected by the agreement, both those being transferred and those retained.

4 A detailed explanation of any specially negotiated exit clauses along with any mid-contract termination periods agreed in advance.

5 Details of any arrangement for the client to benchmark the service and the date when it is to be carried out.

6 The date by which renewal discussions must have commenced before the end of the contract period.

7 Details of any agreement to share the risks and/or rewards.

8 An anticipation of outside factors, such as changes in legislation, that might affect the contract and a framework for dealing with any problems that might arise as a result.

9 An explanation of any indemnity enjoyed by both the provider and the client.

• • • • • • • • • • • • • •

2 Key issues

Special attention should be paid to the following issues.

> all parties to the agreement and all their staff and agents are normally required to respect the confidentiality of the key elements of the contract

Confidentiality

All parties to the agreement and all their staff and agents are normally required to respect the confidentiality of the key elements of the contract. This requirement can continue for a number of years beyond the duration of the original contract.

Payment terms

The service to which the outsourcing contract relates and the charge that will be made for that service must, obviously, be set down in clear and unambiguous detail together with the commencement date and, if it is different, the date from which charges will commence. Invoicing procedures and settlement terms should be clearly set down, along with any agreement allowing increases in charges during the contract period, with a detailed explanation of the inflation index or other basis upon which such increases are made. It is often necessary to estimate payment in the early stages when the amount of work to be performed is, as yet, uncertain. This situation is normally dealt with by the inclusion of a clause detailing how and when any discrepancies should be corrected.

It is likely that, no matter how carefully planned the agreement, during the course of the contract it will be appropriate for the service provider to perform additional services not originally allowed for. This situation should be anticipated with the inclusion in the contract of a formula by which payment for these services may be calculated.

The provider will normally wish to insert a clause requesting that expenses should be paid within a specified period, on presentation of the relevant expense forms and receipts. Such expenses will mainly be those that the client's staff previously incurred themselves in carrying out the transferred service, such as travelling and living expenses.

Procedures

The contract normally includes a clause requesting the provider to attempt, to the best of its abilities, to meet any unexpected increases in workload and changes in target dates that might arise. Such a clause would be very difficult to enforce but it is intended to demonstrate that the provider should react to changes in circumstances in the same way that the client's staff would have done and with the client's best interests at heart.

Most outsourcing contracts will also contain an acknowledgement that changing circumstances over the lifetime of the agreement, often five years or so, will naturally affect the level and type of the service required. The flexibility necessary to adapt to such changes should be built into the contract from the outset. Normally both parties agree that there should be no increase in cost for changes that do not result in an increase in workload. The framework should be in place for agreement to be reached at a suitable level on any changes to the scope of the contract. If the situation changes to the extent that alterations are required to the SLAs or to payment terms laid down in the contract, then suitable amendments should be added to the contract at the earliest possible date.

It may be appropriate, particularly where a partnership arrangement is in place, for a clause to be inserted giving the provider the right to charge for short-term development costs incurred during the contract period. Incurring such costs would require the client's agreement, and would be justified by action taken to improve the service in some way.

Intellectual property

The issue of intellectual property is given a great deal of attention in many contracts. This is natural, since not only will both client and service provider soon be using each other's existing intellectual property, but they will also wish to know whether they have joint ownership of any new developments. Contracts tend not to go into precise detail about the individual elements of such property, instead classifications such as 'software' are normally sufficient.

> generally speaking, the parties to the agreement do not pay each other for intellectual property rights

Generally speaking, the parties to the agreement do not pay each other for intellectual property rights. However, where such rights belong to third parties, care must be taken to ensure that the terms of any existing agreements or licences are not breached.

The right of inspection

It is frequently necessary for the client to enter the site and inspect various elements of work at intervals during the period of the agreement and the right to do so should be set out in the contract. Reasonable access should not be refused, although the provider may request written notice in advance of a visit to the site by the client for any purpose, including internal audit. It is not unknown for providers to insert a clause into the contract allowing them to charge the client for extra and unnecessary work caused by excessive visits.

There can be no change to the right of access of the external auditors, which remains as it was prior to the outsourcing agreement.

Statutory and other obligations

The contract will normally contain a clause obliging all interested parties, including subsidiaries and any subcontractors, to comply with all statutory regulations such as health and safety requirements, by-laws, national and such international laws as apply and any rules previously imposed by the client. Discussions on any unusual rules and regulations relating to the client's business should be held at an early stage of negotiations.

Transferred property

In some outsourcing agreements, the work will be carried out at premises already owned by the service provider. The contract relating to such an arrangement will probably contain a clause requesting the provider to ensure that reasonable security measures are in place. Where the client owns the premises in which the work will be carried out, then it may wish to insert a clause in the contract stating that no changes should be made to the buildings and site without prior notice being given. If the agreement involves leasing or selling the site to the provider, the client should probably consider what the best course of action would be in the eventuality that the agreement has to be terminated, and make provision for this in the contract.

The possibility of claims

The contract will normally contain an agreement that notice will be given in writing as soon as possible of any intent on the part of either of the parties to make a claim against the other. In addition, they will agree that in such an event, any relevant records requested by either party will be made available to the other as rapidly as possible.

The contract will also need to deal with the possibility of a successful claim for negligence against one or both of the parties to the agreement by a third party. It is important that neither client nor provider should suffer a financial loss as a result of negligence on the part of the other. Thus, there will usually be a clause in the contract stating that where the fault lies only with one party, it will indemnify the other against any such claims.

Limitation of liability

It will usually be in the best interests of each of the parties to the contract that liability should be limited for both of them. They will normally agree that any problems should be addressed amicably, avoiding punitive damages where possible. The party at fault should have as much chance as possible to redress the situation and the other party should do its utmost to limit any resulting damage.

Some contracts also include a clause specifying a time period within which any claim must be made. Such a time period will normally commence at the point when the problem has become apparent to both parties.

Dealing with personnel

The contract will normally state that, from a specified transition date, the provider will take over complete responsibility for the staff, including the need to conform to the TUPE regulations and Acquired Rights Directive. It will usually be made clear that responsibility for any actions taken before this date rests with the client. The provider will wish to ensure that any personnel liabilities which become known after the transfer date but which relate to the period before that date fall to the client, whether or not the client knew about them or should have known about them.

It is important that any liabilities for redundancy settlements should be clearly understood. It will normally fall to the client to settle with any employees made redundant prior to the transition. If those redundancies took place after the parties began their negotiations, it will be advisable to explain in detail the action that was taken and ensure that there is no uncertainty about the liability.

The transferred employees must be informed of their new terms and conditions in writing, with clear explanations of any changes. The contract should contain a statement to the effect that this has been carried out. If the client wishes to make any guarantees to the staff being transferred, relating either to their continuation of

> the transferred employees must be informed of their new terms and conditions in writing, with clear explanations of any changes

employment or to their terms and conditions, then these will also need to be precisely documented.

Dealing with pension rights

The TUPE regulations do not go into detail on the issue of pension rights. For this reason, some people feel that the subject can be safely omitted from an outsourcing contract. In practice, however, this is an area which does need to be laid down in careful detail in the contract, due to the long-term nature of any problems which might arise from short-term errors. The fact that each member of staff may have a different pension arrangement means that, in order to cut down on the possible confusion in years to come, full details will need to be given of the actions taken and arrangements made for each transferred individual.

The provider normally requires certain guarantees and assurances

It will normally be in the provider's interests to ensure that the following provisions are included in the contract.

1 An undertaking by the client to provide all the necessary documentation, specialized knowledge and anything else required by the provider in order to fulfil its obligations, without additional charge.

2 The client's guarantee that the information it has provided and on which the provider's bid was based is accurate. This should cover issues such as the ownership and condition of all relevant assets, including intellectual property such as software licences, and also the financial records and payments relating to the transferred staff.

3 An undertaking from the client that, for the period of the contract, it will allocate personnel and managers with the necessary skills to liaise with the provider and, where applicable, provide an acceptable working environment for the provider's staff.

4 An undertaking from the client to make good any breaches of the above clauses at its own expense.

5 Following on from the last point, an agreement that if the provider's performance is affected by serious breaches by the client of any of the above then the provider will have the right to renegotiate or, as a last resort, to cancel the contract.

3 Details of the transition

This part of the contract will usually include the following information.

1 The date and time at which the provider will take over the property, equipment, materials, other assets, software licences, intellectual property and the staff, and the terms under which this transfer will take place.

2 In case of any unanticipated problems relating to the transfer of the above, a framework for deciding on alternative arrangements and for determining who should bear any resulting costs. Problems may arise where insufficient consideration has been given to ownership rights over, for example, software and equipment belonging to third parties.

3 Details of the responsibilities and costs to be borne by the provider for the lifetime of the contract.

4 Details of the responsibilities and costs to be borne by the client for the lifetime of the contract.

Detailing the services to be provided during the transition period

Each contract will be unique but most will include provisions to cover the aspects which follow.

1 Agreements relating to the preparation of staff due to be transferred, including training and counselling, along with any similar assistance to be provided to the staff staying with the client. Arrangements for the transfer of staff records and payroll must also be detailed. A date, before the end of the transition period, will normally be given by which these tasks should be completed. Ideally, this date should be set as early as possible in order to ensure that any problems are ironed out before the transition phase is completed.

2 A detailed description of the service to be performed, service level agreement (SLA) and reporting mechanisms.

3 Details of agreed performance measures and the rates at which any penalties and/or rewards will be calculated.

4 Details, including start and finish dates, of any special projects to be undertaken as an integral part of the transition period. Such projects might include, for example, the implementation of a new ERP system. The estimated costs of the project will probably be set between minimum and maximum levels and there may be specific penalties and rewards relating to the performance of the project.

5 Details and costs of consultancy required during the transitional period for work including, for example, re-engineering. It is normal to cost such consultancy separately from that required at other stages of the contract or for special projects.

6 An undertaking on the part of the provider that if any of the agreed service is to be subcontracted, it will assume full responsibility for the subcontractors' actions and guarantee the standard of performance.

7 If the client wishes to retain the opportunity to veto the appointment of certain staff, then it will be necessary to insert a clause explaining what rights the client has relating to personnel issues.

4 Termination of agreements

> the contract will normally set down those conditions which will need to prevail for the agreement to be terminated before the agreed end date

The contract will normally set down those conditions which will need to prevail for the agreement to be terminated before the agreed end date. These may include:

- insolvency of either party;

- the refusal on the part of either party to abide by the terms previously agreed and set down in the contract;

- non-payment;

- the completion of a key project. For example, if the client's decision to outsource was largely influenced by the prospect of the development of new technology, it may be that once this is in place, the completion of the remainder of the agreement appears less attractive.

All of the above possibilities need to be considered in terms of the consequences for both parties. In the event that a termination of the contract becomes necessary, it will be in the best interests of both parties to ensure that the minimum of time and disruption is required in order to extricate them from the agreement. The amount of the final payment due will depend on what event triggered the termination of the contract. In the last of the examples given above, the client terminates the contract having gained the benefit of the new technology that was its main reason for wanting to outsource. In this case, the provider is likely to seek an additional payment, on the grounds that, rather than the long-term agreement which it believed itself to be involved in, the work it did during the period amounted to little more than consultancy at a lower than normal rate of pay.

The contract must also set down the procedures attendant upon the normal termination of the contract. The provider will usually agree to:

- return the responsibility for the service to the client, or pass it to a third party, with no disruption to the performance of the service.

- allow the client the continued use, under a reasonably priced licence, of software and any other intellectual property necessary for the performance of the service;

- ensure that any confidential material belonging to the client, for which it no longer has a valid requirement, is returned or destroyed;

- evacuate the client's premises, where appropriate, leaving them in a good condition, which should be defined here to avoid any dispute on termination of the contract. The agreement will also usually state that all materials, etc. essential for the continuation of the service will remain, whilst any of the provider's equipment, personnel and materials not required for this purpose are to be removed.

- not recruit staff from the client for a period of time laid down in the agreement.

The client agrees to:

- provide any reasonable assistance required by the provider in returning the service to the client or transferring to a third party;

- ensure that any confidential material belonging to the provider, for which it no longer has a valid requirement, is returned or destroyed. As with the similar undertaking on the part of the provider, it will normally be wise to define such materials clearly in the original contract;

- not recruit staff from the provider for a period of time laid down in the agreement.

- pay for the service until the end of the contract and, at that point, resume control of and responsibility for the service.

Flexibility and the contract

It is usually argued that clients setting too rigid a contract, e.g. 'if you fail to reach any of the following targets the penalty will be X' usually pay more for the services than if the contract had been more flexible. As explained in the main body of the book, this usually happens because a provider considering itself under financial pressure will take every opportunity to improve its profit margin on anything it is required to do that is out of scope.

It is, therefore, essential that the client organization understands the importance of flexibility from the earliest possible moment. To start with it will be necessary to detail what is in scope and which of the related areas are outside the scope. From both parties' point of view, but particularly the client's, it is important that there is no room for doubt in this matter. Only when this has been achieved can adequate pricing levels be agreed for both in scope and out of scope work.

> a plan that requires specified weekly or even daily deadlines will not please many providers

Sometimes the client organization will attempt to limit the chance of failure by producing very detailed plans for both the transition and contract life that stipulate targets that the providers must achieve. A detailed plan will be necessary and should be included in the contract so that there are clear targets for all concerned to aim for and to make it easier for managers to be able to identify reasons for delays. However, a plan that requires specified weekly or even daily deadlines will not please many providers.

A typical compromise is to 'attach' the detailed plan to the contract and make the main targets and the relevant timescales, conditions of the contract.

Clearly, over time, technology is going to change everything done in every business. It may be, therefore, that before the end of five-year contracts which started in 2000, there are significant changes in the accepted state of the art way of carrying out some of the work that is in scope in the contracts. If, in such circumstances, the service provider recommends that the new technology is utilized before the end of the contract, what is the legal and moral situation if an increased charging rate is also requested? Presumably, if it could be shown that it was also in the provider's interest to take up the new technology and if there was no material change to the end product, then a court of law might reason that there was no reason to change the charging basis. However, circumstances are rarely that simple and it might be a factor in the provider's defence if it could demonstrate that it would be disadvantaged in some way by continuing with out-of-date technology.

Obviously, whatever the legal and moral rights and wrongs it would be preferable to avoid confrontation between the parties. Common sense dictates that this will be best achieved if both parties understand the in and out of scope issue and have agreed some flexible basis for out of scope charging.

appendix d

• •

the rights of transferred staff

There is a significant amount of preparation work to be completed before the transfer date in regard to the harmonization of terms and conditions for transferring employees. The extent of this work will depend on the number of people to be transferred and the range of terms enjoyed by these employees. However, the client is likely to benefit from the fact that the successful service provider will almost certainly have experience of other transfers either from outsourcing arrangements or from assisting with company acquisitions and mergers. The provider will be at least as determined as the client that the transfer is effected as smoothly as possible, because on the transfer date any employee problems become the provider's.

> there is a significant amount of preparation work to be completed before the transfer date in regard to the harmonization of terms and conditions for transferring employees

It is important for a client to study the implications of the Transfer of Undertakings (Protection of Employment) Regulations 1981 (TUPE) as soon as outsourcing is seen as a serious option.

The main aim of TUPE is to ensure that both parties to the transfer of employment treat the employees in a fair and reasonable way. The legislation tries to:

- prevent people being made redundant unnecessarily;
- provide adequate counselling and an explanation of what will happen after the transfer;
- maintain the terms and benefits of employment;
- help with essential relocation;
- provide ongoing training; and
- create a reasonable working environment.

TUPE requirements

One effect of the legislation, however, is that set 'rules' have to be taken into consideration. As far as outsourcing is concerned the following TUPE requirements should be noted.

1 The transferor or the transferee, for that matter, can make employees redundant before or after the business is transferred, but only on the grounds of economic, technical or organization reasons entailing changes in the workforce. These grounds are normally interpreted in such a way that the transfer itself should not be the principal reason for the redundancies.

2 It follows, then, that to comply strictly with the regulations, the transferor cannot make staff redundant before the transfer simply because the transferee does not want them. However, the transferee will probably be able to do so after the transfer.

3 If staff are dismissed on the day of transfer, the transferee is responsible for any redundancy payments due.

4 On the transfer, the transferee assumes the responsibilities of the transferor – the principle is that the employee should not be in a less advantageous position than before the transfer. Accordingly, all conditions of employment remain the same, including anything that was previously agreed with a recognized trade union. The transferee can only change these terms with the full and written agreement of the employees affected.

5 The transferor is legally obliged to inform any employees likely to be affected that a transfer of undertakings is contemplated and this should be done at least six weeks before the transfer date.

Difficulties which can arise

On an industry by industry basis, the major service providers probably offer terms of employment that are as advantageous as any group of employers in Europe. Nevertheless, it is important to realize that their basic terms and conditions for transferred staff may differ slightly from what some other employees enjoy. For example, in many of the service provider organizations, there will be individuals, usually called consultants, whose lifestyle will be based on frequent travel to various client sites to act as the main instigators of change. These consultants will probably enjoy a better package than the average employee who has joined as a result of an outsourcing transfer and will mainly be confined to his or her original site. Almost all organizations in both the public and private sectors employ varied grading levels to reward employees with the highest skill levels. Not being included in higher grades has been known to cause unrest amongst some transferring employees. For that reason the service providers should explain their terms and conditions well in advance of the transfer date.

The key factor as far as the TUPE regulations are concerned is that the employees' situation is likely to be no worse after transferring to the service provider. However, in almost all providers, the transferred employees can and do progress through the company according to their abilities. EDS and others can demonstrate that many of their senior people originally joined as a result of an outsourcing transfer.

Difficulties can arise where an employee or groups of employees are rewarded by the transferring employer at significantly higher rates than the provider can justify taking into account seniority, ability or qualification. In these circumstances the two parties must attempt to find a compromise with the employees concerned.

The TUPE and other regulations governing the transfer of staff do not appear to represent an insurmountable barrier to organizations intent on outsourcing. However, they should not be taken lightly, as their interpretation is subject to challenge and change. Since 1997, for example, there have been a number of widely differing interpretations across European courts with the result that some legal experts now doubt that TUPE applies to outsourcing. Obviously, responsible legislators wish to continue to protect transferred staff and accordingly another update to the TUPE regulations has been promised.

> the TUPE and other regulations governing the transfer of staff do not appear to represent an insurmountable barrier to organizations intent on outsourcing

Redundancy issues

There is nothing to prevent the parties to the contract making any arrangements they like regarding which of them pays for the possible redundancies at each stage. However, it is normal for the client to indemnify the service provider for redundancy costs and any TUPE implications arising from the actions necessary to complete the transition, including relocation costs, due as a result of the transfer of services and from any related implementation of new systems. These indemnities will normally cover staffing implications at any of the client's other companies, sites and business functions that might be affected.

The provider's responsibility for any further redundancies normally begins after the transition stage has been completed. Where a shared risk/rewards benefit contract has been agreed, the contract may either allow for the provider to be liable for further redundancy costs or these may be treated as a first charge on the arrangements made.

If at the end of the contract period a new contract is not awarded to the existing provider, then a further transfer of undertakings will be necessary, either to another services provider or back to the client. The TUPE regulations will again apply and any further redundancies will most likely be the responsibility of the transferee. A copy of the TUPE regulations booklet follows:

The TUPE regulations

The Department of Trade and Industry produces a booklet PL 699 (REVISION 4 at the time of writing but REVISION 5 due) which goes into some detail to explain the employment rights on the Transfer of Undertakings (Protection of Employment) Regulations 1981 (S1 1981 No 1794). These have been amended several times, most recently by the Transfer of Undertakings (Protection of Employment) (Amendment) Regulations 1995 (SI 1995 No 2587) and the Trade Union Reform and Employment Rights Act 1993 (TURERA). Further, as yet unpublished, amendments were made to the Transfer of Undertakings (Protection of Employment) (Amendment) Regulations in 1999 and the government intends to have another go at it in 2000.

These Regulations, which are usually termed TUPE for short, implement the European Community Acquired Rights Directive (77/187/EEC), amended by Directive 98/50/EC. The European Union Acquired Rights Directive protects employees from the loss of 'acquired rights' to pensions, seniority and other valuable privileges when they are transferred to another employer.

Rights already conferred by existing employment legislation are not affected by the TUPE Regulations.

The DTI's PL 699 (Rev 4) contains the following Outline of Regulations.

Purpose

The Regulations preserve employees' terms and conditions when a business or undertaking, or part of one, is transferred to a new employer. Any provision of any, agreement (whether a contract of employment or not) is void so far as it would exclude or limits the rights granted under the Regulations.

The Regulations have the effect that:

- Employees employed by the previous employer when the undertaking changes hands *automatically* become employees of the new employer on the same terms and conditions. It is as if their contracts of employment had originally been made with the new employer. Thus employees' continuity of employment is preserved, as are their terms and conditions of employment under their contracts of employment (except for certain occupational pension rights).

- Representatives of employees affected have a right to be informed about the transfer. They must also be consulted about any measures which old or new employer envisages taking concerning affected employees.

Transfers covered by Regulations

The Regulations apply when an undertaking or part of an undertaking is transferred from one employer to another.

Some examples of transfers are:

- where all or part of a sole trader's business or partnership is sold or otherwise transferred;

- where a company, or part of it, is bought or acquired by another, provided this is done by the second company buying or acquiring the assets and then running the business and not acquiring the shares only;

- where two companies cease to exist and combine to form a third;

- where a contract to provide goods or services is transferred in circumstances which amount to the transfer of a business or undertaking to a new employer.

The Regulations can apply regardless of the size of the transferred undertaking. Thus the Regulations equally apply to the transfer of a large business with many thousand employees or of a very small one (such as a shop, pub or garage).

The Regulations apply equally to public or private sector undertakings.

Transfers not covered by the Regulations

The Regulations do *not* apply to the following:

- transfers by share take-over because, when a company's shares are sold to new shareholders, there is no transfer of the business – the same company continues to be the employer;

- transfers of assets only (for example, the sale of equipment alone would not be covered, but the sale of a going concern including equipment would be covered);

- transfers of a contract to provide goods or services where this does not involve the transfer of a business or part of a business;

- transfers of undertakings situated outside the United Kingdom.

Those provisions of the Regulations which relate to dismissal of employees because of the transfer, the duty to inform and consult representatives and the failure to inform and consult them as required, do not apply to employees who, under their contracts of employment, normally work outside the United Kingdom.

Employer's position in a transfer

Under the Regulations, when an undertaking is transferred the position of the previous employer and the new employer is as follows:

- The new employer takes over the contracts of employment of all employees who were employed in the undertaking immediately before the transfer, *or who would have been so employed if they had not been unfairly dismissed for a reason connected with the transfer.*[1] An employer cannot just pick and choose which employees to take on (but see below).

The new employer takes over all rights and obligations arising from those contracts of employment, *except* criminal liabilities and rights and obligations relating to

---

[1] *The effect of the Regulations as interpreted by the House of Lords in Litster and Others v Forth Dry Dock and Engineering Company Limited and another. This judgment implied these words into the Regulations.*

provisions about benefits for old age, invalidity or survivors in employees' occupational pension schemes.

- The new employer takes over any collective agreements made on behalf of the employees and in force immediately before the transfer (see also **Trade union recognition**).

- Neither the new employer nor the previous one may fairly dismiss an employee because of the transfer or a reason connected with it, *unless* the reason for the dismissal is an economic, technical or organizational reason entailing changes in the workforce. If there is no such reason, the dismissal will be unfair. If there is such a reason, and it is the cause or main cause of the dismissal, the dismissal will be fair provided an employment tribunal decides that the employer acted reasonably in the circumstances in treating that reason as sufficient to justify dismissal. If, in this case, there is a redundancy situation, the usual redundancy procedures will apply (see **Redundancy**).

- The new employer may not, unless the contract of employment so provides, unilaterally worsen the terms and conditions of employment of any transferred employee.

- The previous and new employers must inform and consult representatives of the employees (see **Information and consultation**).

Employees' position in a transfer

When an undertaking is transferred the position of the employees of the previous or new employers is as follows.

- An employee claiming to have been unfairly dismissed because of a transfer has the right to complain to an employment tribunal.

- Transferred employees who find that there has been a fundamental change for the worse in their terms and conditions of employment as a result of the transfer generally have the right to terminate their contract and claim unfair dismissal before an employment tribunal, on the grounds that actions of the employer have forced them to resign. Employees may not make this type of claim solely on the grounds that the identity of their employer has changed unless the circumstances of an individual case change and that change is significant and to the employee's detriment.

In both the above cases dismissal because of a relevant transfer will be unfair *unless* an employment tribunal decides that an economic, technical or organizational reason entailing changes in the workforce was the main cause of the dismissal and that the employer acted reasonably in the circumstances in treating that reason as sufficient to justify dismissal. Even if the dismissal is considered fair, employees may still be entitled to a redundancy payment (see **Redundancy**).

For details of how to complain to an employment tribunal (see **Complaining to an employment tribunal**).

● Employees employed in the undertaking immediately before the transfer (*or who would have been so employed had they not been unfairly dismissed for a reason connected with the transfer – see footnote on page 191*) automatically become employees of the new employer, unless they inform either the new or the previous employer that they object to being transferred. In this case the contract of employment with the previous employer is terminated by the transfer of undertaking but the employee is not dismissed. The previous employer may re-engage the employee.

An employee's period of continuous employment is not broken by a transfer, and, for the purposes of calculating entitlement to statutory employment rights, the date on which the period of continuous employment started is the date on which the employee started work with the old employer. This should be stated in the employee's written statement of terms and conditions; if it is not, or if there is a dispute over the date on which the period of continuous employment started, the matter can be referred to an employment tribunal. (For further details, see booklet PL 700 *Written statement of employment particulars* available free from Jobcentres.)

● Transferred employees retain all the rights and obligations existing under their contracts of employment with the previous employer and these are transferred to the new employer, with the exception that the previous employer's rights and obligations relating to benefits for old age, invalidity or survivors under any employees' occupational pension schemes are not transferred. If the new employer does not provide comparable overall terms and conditions, including pension arrangements, an employee may have a claim for unfair dismissal.

Occupational pension rights earned up to the time of the transfer are protected by social security legislation and pension trust arrangements.

Redundancy

Dismissed employees may be entitled to redundancy payments. Employers must also ensure that the required period for consultation with employees' representatives is allowed. More details are in booklets PL 833 *Redundancy consultation and notification* and PL 808 *Redundancy payments*, both available free from Jobcentres.

Entitlement to redundancy payments will not be affected by the failure of any claim which an employee may make for unfair dismissal compensation.

Where there are redundancies and it is unclear whether the Regulations apply, it will also be unclear whether the previous or the new employer is responsible for making redundancy payments. In such cases employees should consider whether to make any claims against both employers.

Trade union recognition

If the transferred undertaking maintains an identity distinct from the remainder of the new employers business, the new employer will be considered to recognize an independent trade union, in respect of employees transferred, to the same extent that it was recognized by the previous employer. If the undertaking does not keep its separate identity, the previous trade union recognition lapses, and it will then be up to the union and the employer to renegotiate recognition.

Information and consultation

Who must be consulted?

These requirements apply in respect of any employees who may be affected by the transfer, whether employed by the new or previous employers. An employer is required to inform and, if appropriate, consult *either* representatives of an appropriate recognized trade union *or* elected representatives of the employees.

An employer who recognizes an independent trade union for collective bargaining purposes is not bound to inform/consult it for this purpose, but if this is not done the employer must inform/consult elected representatives. However, an employer who does not recognize an independent trade union for a particular category of employees who may be affected, may only inform/consult elected representatives. An employer may inform/consult a recognized trade union for one group of employees and elected representatives for another.

Where the employer chooses to inform/consult an independent recognized trade union, the employer must deal with a representative of that union who is authorized by the union to carry on collective bargaining with that employer; that maybe the shop steward, or the district union official, or, if appropriate, a national or regional official.

Where the employer chooses to inform/consult elected representatives, who must be employees of the company, he must take steps to ensure that representatives are elected in good time for information/consultation to be undertaken. There is no statutory requirement for permanent representation; it will be sufficient for an employer to arrange for elections as and when required.

Representatives need not be elected specifically for this purpose; an employer may inform/consult through an existing consultative body whose membership is elected, for example, a staff council, provided that it is appropriate to inform/consult this body on this issue. It would not, for example, be appropriate to inform/consult a committee specifically established to consider the operation of a staff canteen about a transfer affecting, say, sales staff; but it may well be appropriate to inform/consult a committee which is regularly informed or consulted more generally about the company's financial position and personnel matters.

The legislation does not specify how many representatives must be elected or the process by which they are to be chosen. An employment tribunal may wish to consider, in determining a claim that the employer has not informed or consulted in accordance with the requirements, whether the arrangements were such that the purpose of the legislation could not be met. An employer will therefore need to consider such matters as whether:

- the arrangements adequately cover all the categories of employees who may be affected by the transfer and provide a reasonable balance between the interests of the different groups;

- the employees have sufficient time to nominate and consider candidates;

- the employees (Including any who are absent from work for any reason) can freely choose who to vote for;

- there is any normal company custom and practice for similar elections and, if so, whether there are good reasons for departing from it.

What must an employer do?

First, the employer of any employee who may be affected must tell their representatives:

- that the transfer is going to take place, approximately when, and why;

- the legal, economic and social implications of the transfer for the affected employees;

- whether the employer envisages taking any action (reorganization for example) in connection with the transfer which will affect the employees, and if so, what action is envisaged;

- where the previous employer is required to give the information, he or she must disclose whether the prospective new employer envisages carrying out any action which will affect the employees, and if so, what. The new employer must give the previous employer the necessary information so that the previous employer is able to meet this requirement. The information must be provided long enough before the transfer to give adequate time for consultation.

Second, if action is envisaged which will affect the employees, the employer must consult the representatives of the employees affected about that action. The consultation must be undertaken with a view to seeking agreement. During these consultations the employer must consider and respond to any representations made by the representatives. If the employer rejects these representations he/she must state the reasons.

If there are special circumstances which make it not reasonably practicable for an employer to fulfil any of the information or consultation requirements, he/she must take such steps to meet the requirements as are reasonably practicable.

Rights of representatives

Representatives and candidates for election have certain rights and protections to enable them to carry out their function properly. The rights and protections of trade union members, including officials, are in some cases contained in separate provisions to those of elected representatives but are essentially the same as those of elected representatives described below. For further details of the rights of trade union members see booklet PL 871 *Union membership and non-membership rights*.

The employer must allow access to the affected workforce and to such accommodation and facilities, e.g. use of a telephone, as is appropriate. What is 'appropriate' will vary according to circumstances.

The dismissal of an elected representative will be automatically unfair if the reason, or the main reason, related to the employee's status or activities as a representative. An elected representative also has the right not to suffer any detriment short of dismissal on the grounds of their status or activities. Candidates for election enjoy the same protection. Where an employment tribunal finds that a dismissal was unfair, it may order the employer to reinstate or *re-engage* the employee or make an appropriate award of compensation (see also booklet PL 712 *Unfairly dismissed?*). Where an employment tribunal finds that a representative or a candidate for election has suffered detriment short of dismissal it may order that compensation be paid.

An elected representative also has a right to reasonable time off with pay during normal working hours to carry out representative duties. Representatives should be paid the appropriate hourly rate for the period of absence from work. This is arrived at by dividing the amount of a week's pay by the number of normal working hours in the week. The method of calculation is similar to that used for computing redundancy payments (see booklet PL 808 *Redundancy payments* available free from DTI orderline 0870 1502 500).

Complaining to an employment tribunal

The following may complain to an employment tribunal:

- an employee who has been dismissed or who has resigned in circumstances in which they consider they were entitled to resign because of the consequences of the transfer (see **Employees' position in a transfer**). An employee must complain within three months of the date when their employment ended. (The method of calculating this date is explained in booklet PL 712 *Unfairly dismissed?* available free from Jobcentres). It may be unclear whether claims should be made against the previous or the new employer. In such cases, employees should consider whether to claim against both employers. Certain categories of employees are not entitled to claim unfair dismissal; a list of these is given in booklet PL 712 *Unfairly dismissed?*

- an elected or trade union representative, if the employer does not comply with the information or consultation requirements (see **Information and consultation**). A representative must complain within three months of the date of the transfer;

- a representative or candidate for election who has been dismissed, or suffered detriment short of dismissal. A complaint must be made within three months of the effective date of termination (or, in the case of a detriment short of dismissal, within three months of the action complained of);

- a representative who has been unreasonably refused time off by an employer, or whose employer has refused to make the appropriate payment for time off, may also complain to an employment tribunal. A complaint must be made within three months of the date on which it is alleged time off should have been allowed or was taken;

- an affected employee where the employer has not complied with the information or consultation requirements other than in relation to a recognized trade union or an elected representative. A complaint must be made within three months of the date of the transfer.

(In any one of the above cases the tribunal can extend the time limit if it considers that it was not reasonably practicable for the complaint to be made within three months.)

- an employee who wishes to claim a redundancy payment. The application should normally be made within six months of the dismissal (see booklet PL 808 *Redundancy payments*).

The necessary form IT 1, or IT 1 (Scot) in Scotland, for application to a tribunal and explanatory leaflet ITLI can be obtained from local offices of the Employment Service.

If a representative complains to an employment tribunal that an employer has not given information about action proposed by a prospective new employer and if the employer wishes to show that it was 'not reasonably practicable' to give that information because the new employer failed to hand over the necessary information at the right time, the employer must tell the new employer that he or she intends to give that reason for non-compliance. The effect of this will be to make the new employer a party to the tribunal proceedings.

Conciliation

The tribunal will send a copy of the completed form to a conciliation officer of the Advisory, Conciliation and Arbitration Service (ACAS) who will try to promote a settlement of the complaint without a tribunal hearing.

The services of a conciliation officer will also be available in the absence of a formal complaint, if the employee or either employer requests them. In such a case the employee or employer can get in touch with a conciliation officer through an office of ACAS (addresses on p. 12 of the PL 699 (Rev 4) booklet). Information given to conciliation officers in the course of their duties will be treated as confidential. It may not be divulged to the tribunal without the consent of the person who gave it.

Tribunal hearing and awards

If no settlement is reached, the employment tribunal will hear the case. If complaints are upheld, awards may be made against the previous or new employer, depending on the circumstances of the transfer.

Unfair dismissal awards – Employment tribunals may order reinstatement or re-engagement of the dismissed employee if the complaint is upheld, and/or make an award of compensation. Further details are in booklet PL 712 *Unfairly dismissed?*

Detriment awards – The employer may be ordered to pay compensation to the person(s) concerned. The compensation will be whatever amount the tribunal considers just and equitable in all the circumstances having regard for any loss incurred by the employee.

Information and consultation awards – The employer who is at fault may be ordered to pay compensation to each affected employee, up to a maximum of four weeks' pay. If employees are not paid the compensation, they may present individual complaints to the tribunal, which may order payment of the amount due to them. These complaints must be presented within three months from the date of the original award (although the tribunal may extend the time-limit if it considers that it was not reasonably practicable for the complaint to be presented within three months).

Advisory, conciliation and arbitration service

ACAS Public Enquiry Points

Birmingham	(0121) 622 5050	**Liverpool**	(0151) 427 8881
Bristol	(0117) 974 4066	**London**	(020) 7396 5100
Cardiff	(029) 2076 1126	**Manchester**	(0161) 228 3222
Fleet	(01252) 811868	**Newcastle upon Tyne**	(0191) 261 2191
Glasgow	(0141) 204 2677	**Nottingham**	(0115) 969 3355
Leeds	(0113) 243 1371		

ACAS main offices

Midlands Region
Leonard House, 319/323 Bradford Street, Birmingham B5 6ET
Anderson House, Clinton Avenue, Nottingham NG5 1AW

Northern Region

Commerce House, St Alban's Place, Leeds LS2 8HH

Westgate House, Westgate Road, Newcastle upon Tyne NE1 1TJ

North West Region

Boulton House, 17–21 Chorlton Street, Manchester M1 3HY

Cressington House, 249 St Mary's Road, Garston, Liverpool L19 0NF

South and West Region

Regent House, 27a Regent Street, Clifton, Bristol BS8 4HR

Westminster House, Fleet Road, Fleet, Hants GU13 8PD

London, Eastern and Southern Areas

Clifton House, 83–117 Euston Road, London NW1 2RB

39 King Street, Thetford, Norfolk IP24 1AU

Suites 3–5, Business Centre, 1–7 Commercial Road, Paddock Wood, Kent TN12 6EN

Scotland

Franborough House, 123–157 Bothwell Street, Glasgow G2 7JR

Wales

3 Purbeck House, Lambourne Crescent, Llanishen, Cardiff CF4 5GJ

Head Office

Brandon House, 180 Borough High Street, London SE1 1LW

index